BEST AUSSIE SLANG
MACQUARIE

BEST AUSSIE SLANG

MACQUARIE

Published by Macquarie Dictionary Publishers Pty Ltd
Sydney, Australia

First published 2008

Copyright © Macquarie Dictionary Publishers Pty Ltd 2008

Cover design: Natalie Bowra
Illustrations: Simon Goodway
Typeset by Macmillan Publishing Solutions, Bangalore-25
Printed in Australia by McPherson's Printing Group

National Library of Australia Cataloguing-in-Publication entry

Title: Macquarie best aussie slang / editor, James Lambert.
Edition: 1st ed.
ISBN: 9781876429652 (pbk.)
Subjects: English language–Australia–Slang–Dictionaries.
Other Authors/Contributors: Lambert, James.
Dewey Number: 427.99403

All rights reserved. No part of this publication may be reproduced, stored in a retrieval system, or transmitted in any form, or by any means, electronic, mechanical, photocopying, recording or otherwise without the prior written permission of the publisher.

A number of words entered in this dictionary are derived from trademarks. However, the presence or absence of indication of this derivation should not be regarded in any way as affecting the legal status of any trademark.

CONTENTS

Australian slang vii
James Lambert

Macquarie Best Aussie Slang 1

AUSTRALIAN SLANG

James Lambert

General editor
Macquarie Australian Slang Dictionary* and *Macquarie Best Aussie Slang

The words *Aussie* and *slang* go together like *bloke* and *sheila*, like *fair dinkum* and *true blue*. Call it Strine, call it Ocker, call it whatever you like, but the way we speak is at the very heart of our national identity. We are a relaxed country with a healthy dismissiveness of authority and formality, so it stands to reason that the informality of slang has burgeoned here like nowhere else. In fact, you'd have to be bloody un-Australian not to use slang, not to like slang, not to love slang – and this little ripper of a book is a celebration of all that is bonzer in the Australian idiom.

But before we start, let's have a bit of a look at just what Australian slang really is.

Beginnings

Australian slang has one of the longest traditions of any variety of English. It is fair to say that Aussie slang began the very day the ships of the First Fleet left the docks of the Old Dart and set out on the arduous journey Down Under.

The convicts, settlers, soldiers and sailors aboard spoke a mish-mash of differing dialects and versions of British working class slang – all of which were mixed together in a unique medley during the long voyage to the remote shores of distant New Holland.

Words spoken on that trip would have included the familiar and enduring *bloke* and *booze*, the obsolescent *chiack* 'to tease', *rum* meaning 'bad' (which survives in the Tasmanian colloquialism *rum'un* 'a character'), probably *conk* 'the nose', and most definitely the ubiquitous Great Australian Adjective *bloody*.

Much is made of our convict beginnings, especially by foreigners who wish to deprecate us, and it is well established that members of the criminal fraternity did continue their former habits in their new land. One word which began in the shadows of life is the quintessential Australianism *bludger*. This is a shortening of the term *bludgeoner* which referred to a prostitute's pimp who carried a bludgeon to keep his women in line, and no doubt to assist in enforcing payment, or else to out-and-out rob mug clients. The bludgeoner was a cowardly bastard who *bludged* off women and the modern word *bludger* still carries the vitriol of its original application. Other words of convict or underworld origin are *cove*, *nark*, *beak* 'a judge', and *dunny*, the modern descendant of the earlier *dunnekin*.

Dialect influence

Throughout 19th-century Britain – before the days of telecommunications – language changed strikingly from region to region and it was possible to detect where a person came from by the way they spoke English. These different versions of the language are known as regional dialects. During the colonial period large numbers of dialect speakers migrated to Australia, each bringing with them a store of words, phrases and expressions from their own locality – and it is to these that a number of modern Australian slang words owe their origin. Examples include *fair dinkum*, *chook*, *dag*, *billy*, *burl*, *nointer* and *ripper*.

Irish English is of course just another British dialect and Australia saw no small number of immigrants from the Emerald Isle, which fact can be seen today in the word *barrack,* and the very Australian second person plural pronoun *youse* – a variation of the typical Irish *yez,* which owes its existence to the fact that Gaelic had separate forms for the singular and the plural second person pronoun.

Aboriginal influence

When the first white settlers arrived, there were over 300 separate languages spoken by the traditional owners of this country. Sadly most of these languages are now extinct. Naturally the colonists borrowed many words from Aboriginal languages, especially for unfamiliar flora and fauna – *budgerigar, dingo, kangaroo, koala, bindi-eye* and *yabby* – and for items of traditional Aboriginal culture – *boomerang, humpy,* etc. In terms of slang, a number of Aboriginal words were taken and then given slightly different meanings. Thus the *dilly* which was a traditional Aboriginal bag made from native grass twine, in slang becomes a general term for any small bag for bits and bobs. Other notable examples are *bung* 'no good', *cooee, yakka* 'hard work' and *yabber* 'to talk', and from Aboriginal pidgin English we get *the big smoke* and possibly also *jumbuck.*

Native-born slang

As change is a natural and inevitable part of language, so Australian English continued to develop on its own and in its own way – a new shoot cut off, as it were, from its parent plant a world away in the northern hemisphere. Part of this natural growth was the creation of new slang terms. Unique Australian coinages are legion, such as *battler, beaut, bonzer, bottler, chunder, digger, dill, drongo, footy, franger, G'day, grouse, hoon, joey, norks, ocker, perv, ropeable, rort, sanger, sheila* and *wowser*, to name just a few. There are also countless slang phrases, many of which demonstrate the Aussie love of humour, such as *a shingle short, happy little vegemite, London to a brick, map of Tassie, no flies on you, not much chop, no worries, like a shag on a rock, shoot through like a Bondi tram, dry as a dead dingo's donger* and *I hope your chooks turn into emus and kick your dunny down*.

Cockney and rhyming slang

Cockney is the name for the dialect peculiar to the East End of London and is sometimes incorrectly regarded as the precursor to Australian English. In fact, the amount of Aussie slang that can be directly attributed to Cockney is next to nothing. Still, it was in London's East End that rhyming slang first appeared, way back in the 1840s. This new slang phenomenon swept through Britain and within the space of a few decades had made its way to Australia. Very few of the original Cockney rhyming slang terms are still in existence, two notable exceptions being *plates of meat* 'feet' and *elephants* (short for *elephant's trunk*) 'drunk'.

In Australia, the inherent humour of rhyming slang caused it to take off in no uncertain manner and very soon Aussies were coining their own rhyming slang terms. These include *babbling brook* 'cook', *bag of fruit* 'suit', *billy lid* 'kid', *butcher's hook* 'crook', *Captain Cook* 'look', *Dad 'n' Dave* 'shave', *Reg Grundies* 'undies', *Joe Blake* 'snake', *Noah's ark* 'shark' and *optic nerve* 'perv'.

Part of the fun of rhyming slang is to try it out on unsuspecting people and see if they can work out the rhyme. The guessing game is further enhanced by the dropping of the rhyme word – thus calling a shark a *Noah* requires knowledge of the full form *Noah's ark*. This contrivance has led to the interesting situation where some words have lost their rhyme word entirely and are commonly used by the general public in complete ignorance of the fact that they are using rhyming slang.

How many people know that the word *jack* meaning 'a venereal disease' is short for *jack in the box* – rhyming slang for 'pox'? Other examples are *chunder*, short for *Chunder Loo* (an old cartoon character) which is rhyming slang for 'spew', and *Pommy*, short for *pomegranate*, rhyming slang for 'immigrant'.

US influence

Perhaps one of the greatest concerns for lovers of Australian slang is the seemingly endless encroachment by American slang. At any given point in time there are a number of piquant examples, generally adopted by the younger generations, that make the blood of all ridgy-didge blokes and sheilas boil. In the 1960s it was *cool* and *groovy*, and in the 1980s it was *rad* and *humungous*, and, at present it's terms like *sick* meaning 'excellent' and *skanky ho* 'a disreputable woman'. But it is not as bad as some people like to make out.

The influence of American slang has been felt since the days of the gold rush, way back in the 1860s. In fact, the term *bushwhacker* – which virtually screams 'Australian' – is in origin an Americanism! Further words from the US were picked up during both World Wars, and then, with the advent of rock'n'roll, TV, and finally the internet, the floodgates of cultural imperialism have been irrevocably opened.

Still, despite all this, all is not lost – Australian English is in no real danger of being overtaken by American English. The basic reason is that once an American word is adopted into Australian speech it immediately becomes naturalised. Take for instance the terms *ciggie* 'cigarette', *clobber* 'to hit', *dough* 'money', *floozy* 'a loose woman', *jerk* 'a fool', *knock back* 'to refuse', *mole* 'a spy', *on the blink* 'malfunctioning', *ripsnorter* 'amazing thing', *shack up* 'to live together', *suds* 'beer', *wino* 'a drunkard' and *worrywart* 'an inveterate worrier' – who would dare to question the place of these in Aussie slang? Yet each and every one of these began life in the US!

Even the recently adopted word *sick*, meaning 'excellent', has been Australianised. In the US teenagers say *way sick*, but Aussie kids say *fully sick*. The use of *fully* – as an intensifier – is a uniquely Australian invention.

In just which country a certain slang term was invented is an esoteric fact known only to specialists in the field of etymology. Who would guess that *get a wriggle on* is Australian, but *get a wiggle on* is American? Most people think that *Al Capone*, rhyming slang for 'phone', is American, when actually it is an Australianism! In fact, when people are asked to say whether a certain slang term is originally British, American or Australian they tend to get it right about 33% of the time. In other words, people generally have no idea. So before slagging off some term as a hideous Americanism one might do well to make sure it really is one!

But leaving the question of origins aside, people should not forget that new Australian slang is being coined every day – and this more than anything else is what keeps the American influx at bay. Recent additions to the Australian slang vocabulary include *muffin top* 'roll of fat forced out by too-tight jeans', *Toorak tractor* 'a 4WD that never leaves the city', *pov* 'poor'.

Another area in which Aussies have been particularly productive is in slang names for those tight, revealing, men's swimmers. Witness *budgie smugglers* – no-one but an Aussie would have come up with that one! But they also get called *cock jocks*, *dick daks*, *sluggos* and *toolies* – just to name a few.

Basically, Aussies can't help themselves. They just have to come up with new slang terms – it's the Australian way – bugger the Yanks and Poms.

Further solace might also be gained from the fact that some Australianisms are making their way to America! Steve Irwin taught them all to say *Crikey!*, but there are also reports that phrases such as *no worries, onya* and *fair dinkum* are now being used in downtown USA. How long will it be before they'll be saying *silly as a two-bob watch* and *don't come the raw prawn with me*? Don't hold your breath, I suspect.

The future

What of the future? Where are we heading? Well, dear readers, those are questions that only you can answer! It is entirely up to Aussies how their language will develop. What about those dinky-di Aussie words that are dying out? Well, if you are unhappy that you never hear *cobber* and *bonzer* any more – then get out there and start saying them. If you do, others will follow. If you don't give a rats – then so be it. You can't control language by legislation, education, or by whingeing about it – language is what you say, on a day-to-day basis. Speak and ye shall preserve!

A

Acca Dacca a nickname for the undisputed kings of Aussie rock, AC/DC.

aerial ping-pong a derogatory term for Australian Rules football used by followers of the Rugby codes.

after grog bog a particularly noisome excrement produced the morning after the night before. Abbreviated to **AGB**. Also called the **post grog bog** (or **PGB**), the **beer grog**, the **grog bog**, or simply the **groggy**. Keep away!

Albany doctor See **doctor**.

Al Capone rhyming slang for 'phone'. Interestingly, Aussie slang – not American.

the Alice Alice Springs, the capital of the Red Centre.

all alone like a country dunny on your lonesome; totally alone. The traditional Aussie dunny, before the age of septic tanks and town sewerage, was always a stand-alone structure placed well away from the house – for obvious olfactory reasons!

all over bar the shouting finished with, for all intents and purposes.

all over the place like a madwoman's breakfast in complete confusion and disarray. Some would have it that it should be **all over the place like a madwoman's custard**, still others say **knitting**, or **lunch box**, or **washing**. Which shows an amazing versatility in your average madwoman.

all yack and no yakka all talk but no action.

amber fluid a beer lover's word for beer. Also called **amber liquid**, **amber nectar** or just simply **amber**.

ambo an ambulance or an ambulance officer. Aussie slang since the 1990s.

Anzac a soldier from Australia or New Zealand. Originally referred only to Gallipoli campaigners, (the Australian and New Zealand Army Corps), then to all World War I soldiers, and later extended to any Aussie or Kiwi soldiers. It is interesting to note that at the

Anzac

time the word first came about (1915) acronyms were very scarce things. It was the telegraphers who first started to use the shorthand ANZAC. The troops quickly picked the term up and started using it to refer to themselves and to coin names for things in their immediate surrounds, as the **Anzac button**, a bent nail used as a button substitute, **Anzac soup**, a shell hole polluted by a corpse, **Anzac stew**, boiled water with a single bacon rind, and **Anzac wafer**, a hard biscuit issued instead of bread – 'one of the most durable materials used in the war'. On a more positive note we have the term **Anzac spirit** or the **spirit of Anzac**, in other words, courage, tenacity and sacrifice.

the Apple Isle Tasmania, famed for its apple orchards. A Tasmanian is an **Apple Islander**.

arc up to become upset; to bridle or become livid with anger; to 'flare up' – like a welder's torch.

all over the place like a madwoman's breakfast

aristotle rhyming slang for 'bottle'. From Cockney. Hence, in Australia, through a convoluted process, also rhyming slang for 'arse'. The logic goes: aristotle = bottle; bottle and glass = arse; so, aristotle = arse! Sometimes shortened to **aris** or **aras**.

arvo the afternoon. A classic Australian shortening using the *-o* suffix. Been around since the 1920s. You can also use the *-ie* suffix and say **arvie** or **aftie**.

Athens of the South Melbourne – because it has the second largest Greek population of any city in the world, after Athens!

Aunty an affectionate moniker for the Australian Broadcasting Corporation.

aunty arms the arms of an overweight or matronly woman, having flabby triceps.

Aussie 1. Australian, as in *Aussie beer*, *Aussie know-how*, *Aussie English* or *Aussie tucker*. Travellers to America will be amused to hear the Yanks pronounce it *ossy* (rhyming with *bossy*) – which means that they have more often seen the word in print than actually heard it. It is sometimes spelt **Ozzie**, and, even more uncommonly, **Ossie**. 2. an Australian. *There were a couple of Aussies at the bar*. In its widest sense this refers to any citizen of this highly multicultural land, however, contextually it is also commonly used to refer to your typical Anglo-Australian, as opposed to Asians, Islanders or other ethnic Australians. 3. Australia. *I can hardly wait to get back to Aussie*. 4. in the money market it means the Australian dollar. *The Aussie fell against the greenback today*. 5. a type of pizza or hamburger with bacon and eggs.

Aussie battler a typical member of the Australian working class who has to struggle hard to make a decent living. Also affectionately known as the **little Aussie battler**.

Aussie cheer the now traditional sporting cheer for Australian sporting heroes. For the record: 'Aussie, Aussie, Aussie, Oy, Oy, Oy! Aussie, Aussie, Aussie, Oy, Oy, Oy! Aussie, Oy! Aussie, Oy! Aussie, Aussie, Aussie, Oy, Oy, Oy!' Popularised and brought to the rest of the culturally-starved world during the 2000 Olympics.

Aussieland this wide brown land; God's own country; a land girt by sea; Australia by any other name.

Australian salute the movement of the hand and arm to brush away flies from your face. Also called the **Barcoo salute**.

axe handle a rough unit of measurement mostly used by country folk. *It was about six axe handles wide. She was a couple of axe handles across the beam.*

B

babbling brook rhyming slang for 'cook'. Often shortened to **babbler**, or even just **bab**.

backblocks **1.** remote, sparsely inhabited inland country; the sticks. Aussie slang since the 1860s. **2.** the outer suburbs of a city.

back o' beyond the far outback; anywhere remote. Aussie slang since the 1870s.

back of Bourke any remote outback area; the backblocks. Recorded since 1896. Bourke is a town in north-west NSW.

bag **1.** an ugly woman. *My blind date was an absolute bag*. **2.** to criticise harshly; to knock. *Me mates all bagged me for buying the wrong beer*.

baggy green the Australian Test cricket cap. To **don the baggy green** is to represent Australia at Test cricket.

bag of fruit Aussie rhyming slang for 'suit'.

bags a cry by which you establish a right by the mere virtue of having made the first claim, as in *Bags I have first ride* or *Bags the window seat*. As a verb, to reserve by making the first claim. *It's not fair, I bagsed it first!* Generally used by kids. In Queensland you find the term **bar** is also used in this way.

bald as a bandicoot totally bald. Bit of a weird one this, as bandicoots are manifestly furry – not bald.

Bali belly diarrhoea, as suffered by travellers to South-East Asia.

ball huggers speedos. For a full set of synonyms see **sluggos**.

Balmain basketweaver a wealthy inner-city trendy with pretensions to an alternative lifestyle. Also called a **basketweaver from Balmain**. Balmain is a yuppified Sydney suburb.

Balmain bulldozer Sydney slang, a derogatory term for a city-only 4WD. Exactly identical to the **Balmoral bulldozer**. See **Toorak tractor** for a veritable swag of synonyms from around the country.

banana bender a derisive term for a Queenslander. See **cornstalk** for similar terms of derision for people from other states.

B and S a bachelor and spinster ball; a dance held for young people in country areas. Held in a woolshed or out in the open, patrons dress in formal clothing, drink copious amounts of alcohol, and generally end up sleeping outdoors for the night. Circle work – the creation of circular patterns on the ground with the back wheels of the patrons' utes or cars – is an obligatory end of the dance ritual.

Bandywallop an imaginary remote town.

barbed wire Castlemaine XXXX beer. Queensland slang for a Queensland beer.

barbie a barbecue, both the cooking apparatus and the social event. First recorded back in the 1970s.

Barcoo a river in south-western Qld, well represented in Australian slang. The most common term is the **Barcoo rot**, a type of scurvy caused by drought, hard living, and bad water, in which the skin breaks out in sores, scabs, and suppurating eruptions, and is often accompanied by vomiting, nausea, and digestive problems. Then there is the **Barcoo spews**, a distinctive illness once prevalent in the outback, characterised by nausea and vomiting at the sight of food, probably due to cyanobacteria. A **Barcoo lawyer** is the same as a **bush lawyer** (see entry). The **Barcoo salute** is equivalent to the **Australian salute**, the brushing away of flies.

barney an argument or fight. Also found in British dialect, and probably from there, even though it is recorded earliest in Australia. Also used as a verb meaning to argue or fight.

barrack to shout encouragement for a player or team; to support, as in *I barrack for St George – Up the mighty Dragons!* Can also be used outside of sporting contexts, as in *I barracked for Whitlam back in '72.* This dead-set Australianism dates back to the 1890s.

barry 1. a terrible blunder, mistake or poor performance. Shortened form of **Barry Crocker**, rhyming slang for 'shocker', Barry Crocker being the Australian popular entertainer who took the title role in the *Barry McKenzie* films of the 1970s. Also known as a **bazza**. **2.** a westie, bogan or bevan. **3.** an unpopular person; a nerd, dag or geek. Same as a **Neville** or **Nigel**.

bash the spine to sleep. Great Aussie layabout slang since the 1940s – trying to make sleeping sound like hard work.

bastard **1.** originally a person born of unmarried parents, but now used generally to mean an unpleasant or despicable person. As in *Don't let the bastards grind you down*. A term well-loved in Australia since colonisation and still enjoying great popularity. In fact, the overuse of the word here has led to it being used to refer to any person – whether they are a bastard or not. So a bloke might come up to a bunch of friends and say *What have you bastards been up to?* You can even use it affectionately, as in *Poor bastard, wasn't his fault*. **2.** when not applied to a person, a **bastard** is anything that causes difficulty or aggravation, as in *This engine's a bastard*, or *What a bastard of a day, it's 45 in the shade*. If it is raining heavily, then it is *raining like a bastard*. You can even use it adjectivally, as in *That was a bastard thing to do*.

battler See **Aussie battler**.

beaut **1.** good, excellent, wonderful. *You've been beaut, thanks*. *It's a beaut car*. Aussie slang since the 1910s. Also used as an adverb. *She sings real beaut*. **2.** as a noun, an excellent person or thing. *It's an absolute beaut*. Aussie slang since the 1890s. Also common in the cry of praise **you beaut!** (see entry).

beaut ute a ute owned by a ute lover with immaculate duco, polished chrome sparkplugs – you know the type! The sort of ute displayed in **beaut ute competitions**.

beauty **1.** a cry of joy. A shortening of **you beauty!** **2.** something of excellent quality. Also spelt **bewdy**, to represent the dinkum Aussie pronunciation.

beer coat the ability to endure icy cold weather gained from getting so tanked you can barely feel anything.

beer goggles a distorted view of things gained from getting drunk on beer, especially the drunken attraction to less than attractive people.

beer o'clock time for a beer. Generally after work, but it depends on the individual.

bend the elbow to drink beer.

bevan the Queensland term for a flannie-clad, mullet-sporting, unrefined, ill-educated yobbo. Same as a *westie* in NSW, or a *bogan* in WA, a *chigger* in Tasmania, and so on and so forth. Not a complimentary term. Apparently from the name *Bevan*, seen as typical of this type, though of course women can be bevans too. To create compound words, bevan is reduced to the simple **bev**, so you get **bev-curls**, the long trailing locks of their mullets, and **bev-cars**, the type of mean street machine favoured by male bevans. Female bevans are sometimes referred to as **bev-chicks**. And to **bev out** is to idle away time sitting around doing nothing much.

bickie a biscuit. If you are **a few bites short of a bickie**, then you are not very smart. If you have **big bickies**, then half your luck, you are rich.

big smoke the city, or any built-up area, as opposed to the countryside. Originally a word used in Aboriginal pidgin English.

big spit vomit. *He went for the big spit.*

Big Wet the monsoon season in the tropical north.

billy lid rhyming slang for 'kid'.

billyo originally a euphemism for the 'devil' or 'hell' when used in various phrases and imprecations. Thus, to **run like billyo** is the same as *to run like the devil*, or to **go to billyo** is to *go to hell*, in other words, get lost! If something is **off to billyo** it is far away, or a long way off course.

bingo wings the flabby triceps of an overweight or matronly woman.

a bit more choke and you would have started said to someone who has just let out one of those short sharp farts that sound like a struggling starter motor.

bitzer a dog of mixed breed. From the phrase *bits of this, and bits of that*. Also spelt **bitser**.

black aspro a cola soft drink, used as a curative for a hangover. Also called the **black doctor**.

black stump a putative remote region in the far outback. As in *It's out beyond the black stump*, or *He is the biggest drongo this side of the black stump*.

Bleak City a disparaging nickname for the less-than-sunny city of Melbourne.

bleeding dog's eye a meat pie with tomato sauce.

blind Freddy could see that that's obvious.

blind mullet a tube of excrement floating in the water you are swimming in. Also called a **blind trout** or a **brown trout** or a **pollywaffle**. In Sydney these also go by the name of **Bondi cigar** or **Bondi shark**, and in Victoria you will find, if you're unlucky, the **Werribee trout** or the **King River prawn**.

Blinky Bill rhyming slang for 'dill'. After the well-known koala character created by Australian children's author Dorothy Wall in 1933.

blister 1. a parking infringement attached to a car window. 2. Aussie rhyming slang for 'sister'.

block the head, used only in the phrases **lose** or **do your block**, to lose your temper, and **knock someone's block off**, to thump them mightily in the head.

blockies in Qld, Vic and Tas, circuits of a street block in a car for the purpose of entertainment. *We spent a few hours doing blockies.* Compare **bog laps, lappies**.

bloke general slang word for a man, especially a man's man, a down-to-earth man without pretensions. In Australia, a **good bloke** is one of the highest accolades that can be bestowed. Slightly lower on the scale is a bloke who is **not a bad bloke**. A real bad bloke is a 'bastard'.

blokette a woman who can hold her own with the blokes. *Champion blokes and blokettes dropped their daks for some naked bungee jumping.*

bloody a word used to add emphasis in signifying approval, as in *bloody beauty*, or disapproval, as in *bloody bastard*. It can also be inserted in the middle of words, as in *abso-bloody-lutely*, or *vege-bloody-mite*. Formerly the iconic Australian swearword, so prevalent that it was known as the *great Australian adjective*. There have even been poems written to it. Used to be considered extremely taboo and never to be used in polite society, and accordingly gave rise to many euphemisms as *blooming, bleeding, blinking, flaming, plurry* and *ruddy*. Nowadays it has lost its former glory. A weary, worn-out, ageing prize fighter, no longer packing a punch. Lost its championship belt to that vicious upstart, the F-word, back in the 1960s.

bloody oath! too bloody right! my word! no two ways about it! Also heard as **blood oath!**

blowie a blowfly. These annoying pests have been so called since the 1900s.

blow-in a derogatory term for a visitor or newcomer, especially one who is not going to stay. Aussie slang of the Great Depression, during which itinerants were looked upon unfavourably by locals who were already having trouble scraping by without the added burden of newcomers.

bludge **1.** to waste time when you should be doing something; what the Americans call loafing. **2.** to cadge, as in *Can I bludge a ciggy off you?* To be **on the bludge** is to be actively engaged in bludging. **3.** to **bludge on** someone is to impose on them or live off their hospitality. Strange to say, **bludge off** has exactly the same meaning. **4.** any job which requires next to no work. *This class is an absolute bludge.*

bludger **1.** someone who imposes on others, evades responsibilities, or does not do their fair share of work. It originally meant a low scoundrel living on the earnings of a prostitute, in other words, a pimp. **2.** any person (without any negative sense). *What are you bludgers up to? The poor bludger doesn't know any better.*

blue **1.** a fight, dispute or row. You can **bung on a blue**, **stack on a blue** or **turn on a blue**. Hence, as a verb, to fight or argue, as in *There's no sense blueing over it.* Been around since the 1940s. **2.** an error. Also around since the 1940s. **3.** a nickname for a bloke with red hair. Typical Aussie irony. A little earlier, since the 1930s. **4.** a blue flyer kangaroo.

blue bomber See **brown bomber**.

blue can a can of Fosters beer. As opposed to a **green**, **red**, **white** or **yellow can** (see entries).

blue swimmer a ten dollar note, the colour of which resembles the well-known crab.

bluey **1.** historically, a rolled blanket, originally blue, containing the possessions carried by a traveller through the bush; in other words, a swag. Hence, to **hump the bluey** was to lead the life of a swagman. **2.** a nickname for a red-headed person.

boardies boardshorts. Favoured by surfies, who would never be seen dead wearing **clubbies** (see entry).

boasters speedos – alluding to their revealing nature. For a full set of synonyms see **sluggos**.

boatrace **1.** rhyming slang for the 'face'. **2.** a competition between teams of beer drinkers to see which team can drink its beer the fastest. The teams line up on either side of a long table, facing one another, and the drinking starts at one end and progresses to the other, the rule being that you are not allowed to begin drinking until the teammate next to you has finished.

Bob's your uncle everything is okay. Used in both Australia and Britain, but who the original uncle Bob was remains a mystery.

bodgie **1.** of poor quality, second-rate, as in *a bodgie repair job*. **2.** false; phoney; fake. *She gave the cop a bodgie name*. **3.** In the 1950s and 60s, a **bodgie** was a type of young hooligan or lout that was the terror of refined society. Their girlfriends were **widgies**. Basically, they were disaffected youths who rejected the stodgy morality and world view of the time, slept around a lot, drove motorbikes and fast cars, got pissed and fought, and indulged in petty crime. Clotheswise they were influenced by American fashions of the day, wearing long draping, waistless, leather jackets, and stovepipe jeans or pants. They later morphed into **sharpies** – which was the same thing, but with a different name.

bodgie up to mock up or fake. *The photos had been bodgied up.*

bog an act of defecation. As in *going for a bog* or *hanging a bog*. Hence, as a verb, to defecate – which the Oxford English Dictionary of 1885 exquisitely defined as 'to exonerate the bowels'. In Britain, the **bog** is the toilet, and this usage has some currency in Australia, but is not as common as our usual *dunny*, *loo* or *toot*.

bogan **1.** especially among schoolkids, a fool or idiot. Popular in the 1980s. Perhaps from the *Bogan* River in NSW, as a place from which unsophisticated country bumpkins hail. **2.** in WA and Victoria, a lout or hooligan, especially of a particular social group noted for wearing flannos, black jeans and desert boots; same as the NSW **westie** or the Qld **bevan**. **3.** in Tasmania, a rough lout or hooligan; in Hobart, equivalent to a **chigger**.

bog in to tuck into a meal. A bit of genuine Aussie English from as early as 1917.

bog laps in WA, circuits of a street block in a car for the purpose of entertainment. *Those kids are out there doing bog laps again.* Compare **blockies**, **lappies**.

bomb 1. an old, crappy car; a car that has been flogged to death. An original and genuine Australianism. Now also used in the UK and the US. 2. a jump into water with the knees tucked into the chest and the arms clasped about the knees so as to make an enormous splash and annoy nearby swimmers. As a verb, to jump into the water in this manner. Generally banned but not illegal.

bommie laconic Aussie shortening of *bombora*, a submerged, or partly-submerged, off-shore reef or rock shelf over which waves break.

Bondi chest the puny chest of a weakling. Because Bondi is 'far from Manly'.

Bondi cigar a floating piece of human excrement in the ocean. So called because a major Sydney effluent outlet was located near Bondi beach. Also called a **Bondi shark**. See **blind mullet** for a swag of synonyms.

bonzer great, excellent, terrific. Occasionally spelt **bonza**.

boofhead an idiot; a stupid fellow with an oversized head; a fathead. Been around since the 1940s where it was popularised by the cartoon character *Boofhead* appearing in the Sydney *Daily Mirror* from 1941.

boofy 1. of men, brawny but a bit thick. *I'm sick of all the boofy boys in the gym.* 2. of the hair, having lots of volume.

boogie a piece of nasal mucus, especially one that has come out into the world, as in *Hey drongo, you got a boogie on your top lip*. Also, **booger**.

boomer 1. something impressive; a great success; a beaut. 2. a large, crashing wave. 3. a large, mature kangaroo. Originally a Tasmanian term, dating back to the 1830s; from the same source as the other senses, but influenced by the *booming* sound of the kangaroo's hop. 4. a hoon in a hotted-up car with a booming sound system.

boomerang a borrowed item that the lender stipulates must be returned. *Yes, you can borrow my copy, but remember – it's a boomerang.*

boomerang bender a teller of tall stories.

boot **1.** a kick, as in *Watch yourself or you'll get a swift boot up the Khyber* (*Pass*). To **put the boot in** is to attack unmercifully. This phrase is a genuine Australianism from the 1910s. **2.** rejection or ejection; dismissal from employment. *I got the boot after donging the boss.*

booze bus a mobile police unit used for random breath tests.

booze cruise an outing on a boat which stops at various wharves while the participants patronise a local pub; a pub crawl via water.

booze-up a drinking session.

bo-peep a peek. *Have a bo-peep at that!*

borrie Victorian slang for number twos. Originally referring to Lake Borrie, the largest settling and filtration pond of the Werribee Sewage Farm. The term has now spread to NSW.

boss the male owner of a rural property or station, traditionally responsible for running the property outside the homestead, which is run by the **Missus**.

boss cocky **1.** the top bloke in an organisation; the person running the joint. In rural areas, a station owner or manager. **2.** also used in a negative way for an upstart who lords it over others; a little authoritarian git.

bottler something absolutely brilliant. *You little bottler!*

bottlo a bottle shop.

bowlo a bowling club. Chiefly an eastern states word.

boys in blue the police force.

bread and duck under the table an answer to the question 'What's for dinner?'

brekkie breakfast.

brewer's droop alcohol-induced sexual impotence in men.

Bris-Vegas Brisbane. Partly with ironic reference to Brisbane's lack of showy opulence, and partly because Brisbane was the first Qld city to have a casino. Inhabitants of this fair town are, of course, **Bris-Vegans**.

Bronte buggy Sydney slang, a derogatory term for a 4WD that never sees off-road driving. See **Toorak tractor** for a host of synonyms.

brown bomber a parking inspector. Chiefly used in NSW and SA, but now dying out as the uniform has changed. In

brown sandwich

SA you can find the term **sticker licker**. Vic has the **grey meanie** and the **grey ghost**, the latter also found in NSW and WA. In any area where the uniforms are blue the term has become **blue bomber**.

brown sandwich a bottle of beer. Common slang term in Qld.

brown trout faecal matter floating in your swimming water. See **blind mullet** for a swag of synonyms.

Buckley's chance no chance at all. Possibly referring to a famous escaped convict William Buckley, although the said Buckley did manage to elude the authorities for some 32 years by living with Aborigines before giving himself up, so it seems that he had a pretty fair chance after all. Sometimes the phrase is expressed as **You've got two chances – Buckley's and none**. This is a pun on a well-known Melbourne department store *Buckley and Nunn*.

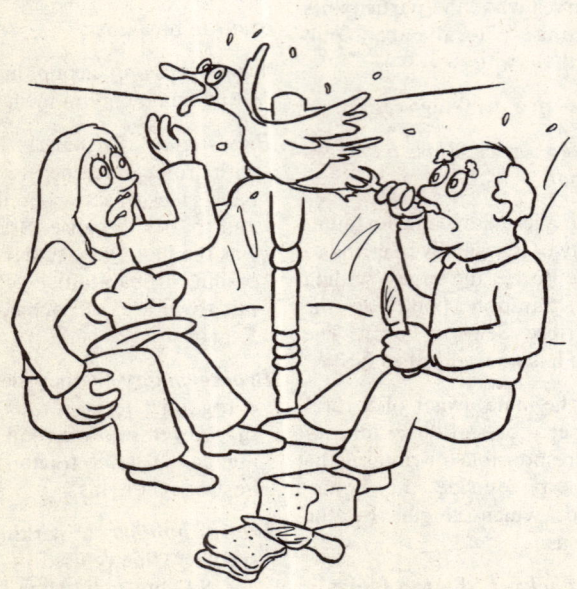

bread and duck under the table

budgie smugglers speedos; sometimes used to mean male underwear. Occasionally also called **budgie huggers**. For a full set of synonyms see **sluggos**.

bugger 1. in Classical Ocker a **bugger** is a person. However, it is not as simple as that – it all depends on how you use it. For example, you can use it in a completely disparaging way to refer to your most hated enemy. *Don't you dare show your face around here ever again, you miserable bugger.* Or, you can use it more gently, as to refer to mildly annoying little kids (*little buggers*), or someone who's a bit wanting in the brains stakes (*He was a stupid bugger, wasn't he?*). In fact, you can even use it about someone you like. *He was a nice old bugger.* 2. when not referring to people, a **bugger** is a nuisance or difficulty, or something unpleasant or nasty, as in *That recipe is a real bugger* or *It's a bugger of a day.* 3. as a verb, to ruin or wreck, as in *That's buggered it!* Or to bamboozle, as in *Well, that buggers me!* Or that common expression of personal ignorance, *Buggered if I know!* 4. as an exclamation, damn! blast! As in *Bugger him, I'm going home.* Or when you drop your Vegemite toast and it lands face down on the floor, *Bugger!* 5. to **play silly buggers** is to muck around.

bugger-all very little; nothing. *He's done bugger-all all day.*

buggered 1. tired out; exhausted. 2. broken; wrecked. 3. damned. *I'm buggered if I'll do that.*

buggerlugs a mock abusive term, used affectionately.

bug rake a hair comb.

builder's crack bum cleavage appearing above the top of the pants. Also called the **builder's smile**.

build-up in the tropical north, the approach of the Wet. You will experience a gradual increase in heat and humidity causing extreme tension and irritability. Also called the **suicide season**, and sometimes leading to **mango madness**.

Bullamakanka an imaginary remote town; any remote place.

Bundy 1. the Qld town of Bundaberg. 2. Bundaberg rum.

bung not in good working order; busted; injured. Borrowed from the Australian Aboriginal language Yagara of the Brisbane region. To **go bung** originally meant to die, but now means to break down, fail, become bankrupt, that kind of thing.

bung it on to behave temperamentally; to put on a display of bad behaviour. Also, to put on airs and graces.

bung on to put on a party or event. *We're bunging on a barbie for our eldest*. If you **bung on an act**, then you make a big fuss over nothing. And to **bung on side** is to behave in a pompous and overbearing manner.

bunny 1. a fool or dupe; a gullible person; an easy victim. 2. a person who accepts the responsibility for a situation. 3. in cricket, a poor batsman. Also called a **rabbit**. Neither of which are as bad as being the **ferret** (see entry). 4. to **shoot a bunny** is to fart.

bunyip aristocracy a derogatory term for what passes for peerage in Australia.

Burnside warrior Adelaide slang, a derogatory term for a city-only 4WD. Also called a **Burnside bus**. See **Toorak tractor** for a host of synonyms.

burr up to become livid with anger. This is a term more common in the Top End and Far North Qld.

bush the great Australian native vegetation. The soul of this highly urbanised nation. Hence, uncultivated or unsettled country; the country as opposed to the city. Thus, to **go bush** is to visit the country, either for a short while, or more permanently, to turn your back on civilisation.

bush bashing the same as **scrub bashing** (see entry).

bush bellows a hat used to fan a camp fire.

bush blow the ejection of snot through one nostril while closing the other off with a finger. Also called the **bushman's hanky**.

the Bush Capital Canberra.

bushfire blonde a redhead.

bushie 1. a person who lives in or comes from the country. A person wise to the ways of the bush; a person adept at living in the bush; a person having exceptional bushcraft. Some city slickers view bushies as unsophisticated country bumpkins, but what would they know? 2. a member of a volunteer bush fire brigade.

bush lawyer a person without legal qualifications but who has a good knowledge of the law and is crafty in applying it.

bushman's breakfast a piss and a good look round; that is, no breakfast at all. Sometimes called a **dingo's breakfast**.

bushman's hanky the act of blowing nasal mucus through one nostril while closing the other off with a finger. Also called a **bush hanky**.

bush mechanic a person skilled in keeping busted old bombs going in the outback, through lateral thinking and crafty ingenuity.

bush oyster the product of a bush blow.

bushranger 1. Australian for highwayman. The Dick Turpin of Down Under. One of a bunch of enterprising young men who thought they could make a living holding up coaches and travellers and decamping into the bush. Noted for yelling 'Bail up!' and 'Stand and deliver!' Most of them came to sticky ends. Terrors of the colonial countryside and the stuff of legends. 2. any unscrupulous bastard who rips you off.

bush telegraph the outback rumour mill. Also, called the **bush wire** or **bush wireless**. A message sent via this system is a **bush telegram**.

bush telly a campfire, or the stars – in other words, what you watch for entertainment at night in the bush.

bush tucker 1. simple fare, as eaten by one living in the bush – damper, tea, kangaroo-tail soup, that sort of thing. 2. food gathered from nature in the bush, as traditional Aboriginal foods.

Bush Week a fictitious week when country people come to town. Used only in the phrase *What do you think this is – Bush Week?* In other words 'What do you take me for – a fool?'

bushwhacker a person living in the bush; a bushie; often viewed as unsophisticated. Not that you'll like to hear this, but this term originated in the US. Yep, way back in 1809, Washington Irving wrote about bushwhackers, some 80 years before the word first appears in Australia. It is obsolete in the US now, having been replaced by *backwoodsman*.

busy as a one-armed paperhanger in a gale extremely busy; too busy to spit.

butcher's canary a blowfly.

butcher's hook 1. rhyming slang for 'look'. Commonly shortened to **butchers**, as in

butcher's hook

Give us a butchers at that. **2.** rhyming slang for 'crook', as in ill, unwell. Also shortened to **butchers** as in *I'm feeling a bit butchers today.* **3.** Can also be used for 'crook' meaning angry, especially in the phrase **go butcher's hook at**. The short form **butchers** is seen in expressions like *No need to go butchers at me.*

BYO **1.** bring your own. A great Aussie entertaining tradition. *We're having a barbie next Saturday, but it's BYO meat and drinks.* **2.** a restaurant which allows clients to bring their own booze.

C

Cabbage Garden an old derisive nickname for Victoria, sneering at its smallness. New South Welshmen reckoned you could put the whole of Victoria inside the backyard of a New South Wales sheep station. Also sometimes called the **Cabbage Patch** or **Cabbage State**. A Victorian was a **cabbage gardener**, **patcher** or **stater**. See **cornstalk** for similar terms of derision for people from other states.

cackle berry a chook's egg.

cactus ruined, kaput. *We aren't going anywhere, the engine's cactus.* Someone in trouble is said to be **in the cactus**. No doubt referring to the dreaded prickly pear which once covered so much of the country, at least, before being eaten holus bolus by the **cacto**, the wondrous *Cactoblastis cactorum* moth, introduced as a biological control.

Cadbury a person who can't handle their drink. That is, they only need 'a glass and a half' to get drunk.

call God on the big white telephone to vomit into a toilet bowl, especially from having drunk too much alcohol.

camp as a row of tents exaggeratedly camp. When this metaphor won't suffice you can crank it up by saying **camp as a row of pink tents**.

cane toad a player for the Queensland state team in the Rugby League State of Origin football competition. Hence, any Queenslander. As opposed to a **cockroach**.

Captain Cook Aussie rhyming slang for a 'look'. Also shortened to **Captain**.

carcass your body or yourself. When directing a guest to a chair it is the height of ocker decorum to say: *Park your carcass, mate!*

cark it to die; to collapse; (of a machine, engine, vehicle, etc.) to fail or break down.

carn a sporting barracker's cry. *Carn the Blues!* The phonetic descendant of 'Come on!' Superlative ocker dialect from the 1960s onwards.

catch and kiss a derisive term for soccer, used by aficionados of the other football codes.

cattle dog Aussie rhyming slang for 'catalogue'.

cellar dwellers the team at the bottom of the competition table.

chalkie a schoolteacher. Since the 1940s.

Charlene the female counterpart of the male westie, bevan or bogan; a bev-chick. Sometimes called a **Charmaine**.

charlie a girl or woman. From rhyming slang *Charlie Wheeler* for 'sheila'. Aussie slang since the 1940s. Charles Wheeler was an artist who painted nudes.

chateau cardboard cask wine. Also called **chateau d'cardboard**.

cheese and kisses rhyming slang for 'missus', that is, the wife.

chew-'n'-spew a fast-food joint.

chiack to taunt or tease; to stir. Also spelt **chiak** or **chyack**.

chick magnet a man who is attractive to many women.

chief cook and bottle-washer the person in charge and doing every other thing as well.

chigger the Hobart term for a westie, bogan or bevan. From the suburb of Chigwell. Also spelt **chigga**.

china a mate. From rhyming slang *china plate*. Originally Cockney, from the 1880s, but used in Australia for many a year.

chippie a carpenter.

chocker completely full; packed or overcrowded. *The hall was chocker.* Hence, replete with food; stuffed.

chocolate soldier 1. in World War I, a member of the AIF's 8th Infantry Brigade, also known as *Tivey's chocolate soldiers*, or *Tivey's chocs*, after Major General Edwin Tivey. Originally a derisive name, but after this brigade saw action, the title was conferred with honour. 2. in World War II, a term of contempt for a member of the Australian Military Force, which was a national militia whose purpose was the defence of Australian territory, and thus did not fight overseas.

choof off to depart.

chook 1. a domesticated chicken. *The chooks got out last night and it took me half an hour to round them all up again.* Classic Australianism, first recorded in 1900. A formerly common greeting was **How are**

your mother's chooks? It didn't require an answer. To **run around like a headless chook** is to behave in an erratic manner. To wish ill luck upon someone you need merely utter **I hope your chooks turn into emus and kick your dunny down**. **2.** a woman, especially an elderly woman. Can be used affectionately, as in *She's a nice old chook*, or in the opposite manner, *Ah, ya silly old chook*.

chook chaser a derogatory term for a trail bike or other small road motorcycle, or for a person who rides such a bike.

chookie a person who drives around the block multiple times for an evening's entertainment. Such laps are called **chookie laps**.

chop shop a panelbeater's.

chuck **1.** to do or perform right away. In Australia certain things are 'chucked' rather than 'done' or 'taken'. For instance, when driving you almost invariably *chuck a U-ie*, or *chuck a left* or *right*. If you jump into a pool in order to make an enormous splash, you *chuck a bombie*. Also, *mentals, wobblies, spazzes, nanas, mickeys* and *willies* are all chucked. **2.** to vomit. *He chucked on my new carpet*. Hence, as a noun, vomit, as in *I made him clean his chuck off my new carpet*. **3.** to stop; be rid of. *I smoked for years before I decided to chuck it*.

chuck a lap to drive around the block as a form of entertainment. *The hoons spent Saturday night chucking laps and screaming out at chicks*. Since this is nearly always done off the main street it is also called **chucking a mainy**. In Whyalla, a hoon around the beach is **chucking a beachie**.

chuck a micky to throw a tantrum; to bung on a show. Truth be known, Aussies don't really approve of people losing their temper – it is seen as overreacting and this phrase is meant to belittle the behaviour. In fact, there is a veritable plethora of put-downs on this same theme, including **chuck a mental, chuck a nana, chuck a spaz, chuck a willy** and **chuck a wobbly**.

chunder **1.** to vomit. First appearing in the 1950s. From rhyming slang *Chunder Loo* 'spew', referring to the cartoon character drawn by Norman Lindsay in a series of advertisements. The fanciful notion that it is a clipping of the nautical cry *Watch under!* used to warn the lower decks when someone from the upper decks was vomiting over the side, is nothing but a silly story.

chunder daks 2. among surfies, to be roughly battered about by a wave. *I got chundered by a massive wave*.

chunder daks someone with their pants pulled right up.

circle work the creation of circular skid marks with the tyres of a motor vehicle. A rural male ritual entertainment.

CJs speedos. Standing for **cock jocks**. For a full set of synonyms see **sluggos**.

Clayton's false, existing in name only, as in a *Clayton's choice*, or a *Clayton's pay increase*. This word had a great vogue in the 1980s due to a long-running TV ad campaign featuring Jack Thompson. Clayton's is an alcohol-free drink, and as Jack kept reminding us, it's 'The drink you have when you're not having a drink'.

clubbie a member of an organised surf-lifesaving club.

clubbies speedos. Favoured by surf lifesavers, as opposed to surfies, who wear **boardies**. For a full set of synonyms see **sluggos**.

cluey smart, shrewd, well-informed.

cluster busters speedos. For a full set of synonyms see **sluggos**.

the Coathanger the Sydney Harbour Bridge. A quaint metaphor in use since the 1940s.

cobber a mate, friend, pal or buddy. Began life in Australia in the 1890s. Formerly in wide and common use. Today still quite common as a form of address in Tasmania. Also shortened to **cob** (since the 1960s). Most likely to come from the Suffolk dialect word *cob* 'to take a liking to'. Others have suggested origins in Yiddish and Aboriginal languages, but these seem less likely.

cobber dobber a person who informs on a mate.

cockatoo a lookout who keeps watch during some illegal activity, such as a two-up game. Hence, as a verb, to act as lookout. So called in reference to the sulphur-crested cockatoo which is known for its habit of posting 'sentries' to noisily warn the feeding flock of any approaching danger. Classic Aussie slang dating as far back as 1827.

cockatoo farmer a small-scale farmer. More commonly called a **cocky**.

cockeyed bob in WA and NT, a particularly violent storm or squall. Different to a **willy-willy** (see entry) which is a dry wind and generally less powerful and destructive.

cock jocks speedos. Politely abbreviated to **CJs**. For a full set of synonyms see **sluggos**.

cockroach a player for the New South Wales team in the Rugby League State of Origin football competition. Hence, any person from NSW. As opposed to a **cane toad**.

cocky 1. a cockatoo, or other parrot. After a big night out you invariably wake with a **mouth like the bottom of a cocky's cage**. 2. a small-scale farmer. 3. a lock of hair sticking up, looking like a cockatoo's crest. 4. a cockroach. Also, **cockie**.

cocky on the biscuit tin the Arnott's Biscuits logo consisting of a rosella-like parrot eating a cracker, which has appeared on tins of Arnott's biscuits since the early 20th century. Used metaphorically to denote being ostracised or left out, that is, being on the outside looking in.

cod jocks speedos. For a full set of synonyms see **sluggos**.

cog 1. a hoon who likes driving noisily around the block multiple times for entertainment. A term in use in the Hunter Valley region of NSW and also in Tasmania. Also called a **cogger** or **cog head**. 2. as a verb, to drive around a block of the main street in a town; to chuck laps. *We were out cogging the other night.*

coin slot bum cleavage appearing above the top of the pants.

coldie a nice cold glass, bottle or can of beer. Been around since the 1950s. Also known as a **cold one**. *Let's have a few cold ones before going home.*

Collins Street cocky in Victoria, a person who owns a country property, often for purposes of tax avoidance, but who lives and works in Melbourne. See **Pitt Street farmer**, **Queen Street bushie**.

come a gutser 1. to suffer a heavy fall, as from a horse. 2. to fail badly; to flop.

come in on the grouter to arrive after the work's finished, either through luck or contrivance. Hence, to be lucky, to have things fall your way.

come in, spinner! 1. in two-up, a call made to signify that all the bets are laid and it is time to spin the coins. 2. a phrase used to inform someone that they have just been successfully duped.

compo workers' compensation.

conk the nose. Also spelt **konk**. First recorded in a glossary of Australian convict slang back in 1812. Common in British and American English in the 19th century, but no longer used in either.

conk out 1. to break down: *The engine's conked out again.* 2. to collapse from exhaustion or the like.

convict a derogatory term for an Australian – used by Yanks, Kiwis, Poms and the like. Referring to our penal beginnings.

cooee the great Australian bush contact cry. Adopted by the first European colonists from the Sydney Aborigines. To not answer the call of *cooooo-eeee* is un-Australian. That's of course if you are **within cooee**. Metaphorically, if you are close to achieving a goal you are **within cooee**, and on the other hand, if you are far from an achievement, you are **not within cooee**.

cop to get or receive. As in *She copped more than her fair share* or *He copped a $200 fine.* To **cop a feel** is to be allowed some sexual fondling by a partner. The phrase *Cop this!* is a polite ockerism uttered before jobbing someone unmercifully. To **cop a gong** is to be awarded a medal. Cop can also mean to accept resignedly, put up with or take, as in *He could dish it out but he couldn't cop it* and *You wouldn't find me copping a deal like that.*

cop it sweet to endure or put up with without complaint.

Corner Country the region where the borders of Qld, SA, and NSW meet. Also, called **the Corner**.

cornstalk a derisive nickname for a person from New South Wales. Similar derisive nicknames for inhabitants of other states are **banana bender** – Queenslander, **cabbage gardener** or **gumsucker** – Victorian, **croweater** – South Australian, and **sandgroper** or merely **groper** – West Australian.

cossie a swimming costume. Chiefly used in NSW. Also spelt **cozzie**.

cot case someone who is exhausted, drunk, or in some way incapacitated, and fit only for bed. In use since the 1930s.

country dunny a traditional rural toilet, consisting of a small shed furnished with a lavatory seat placed over a sanitary can, or a pit, located a decent distance from the house. Hence, to be **all alone like a country dunny** is to be totally alone. An extremely incompetent person **couldn't catch a fly in a country dunny**.

a couple of lamingtons short of a CWA meeting stupid; lacking a full complement of intelligence. For similar comparisons see the entry for **short of**.

cow **1.** a contemptible person. Aussie slang since the 1890s. *You miserable cow.* **2.** a bad-tempered woman. *She was a mean old cow.* **3.** something unpleasant or annoying. *That's a cow of a thing to say. I've had a cow of a day.*

cow cocky a small-scale cattle farmer.

cow-pat lotto a form of lottery in which a cow is placed in a pristine paddock which has been divided into squares which are numbered and raffled off. The winner is decided by the fall of the first cow-pat.

crack a tinnie to open a can of beer.

crikey! a euphemism for the blasphemous exclamation *Christ!* Not exclusively Australian, but taken on board by Aussie swearers with great

cow-pat lotto

gusto. The late crocodile hunter Steve Irwin brought this oath to the attention of Americans who now think we all go around saying *Crikey!* all day.

crook 1. sick. *I'm feeling real crook*. Hence, injured. *Her crook leg is keeping her up at nights.* 2. bad; inferior. *That food was crook*, *He did a pretty crook job.* 3. a criminal; a thief or swindler. Originally US slang from the 1870s, now Standard English. Hence, as an adjective, dishonest or illegal; of an item, stolen. This second usage is an Australian original, and not used elsewhere except New Zealand. 4. angry, annoyed, upset. To **go crook on** someone is to scold them.

crook as Rookwood extremely ill. A bit of an exaggeration as it refers to Rookwood Cemetery in Sydney.

cross-country ballet a derisive term for Australian Rules football. Not to be confused with **cross-country wrestling**, that is, Rugby League or Union.

crow Used in some slang phrases, such as **the land where the crow flies backwards**, meaning any remote outback place. **As the crow flies** relates to a measure of distance in a straight line, as opposed to taking the road. To **draw the crow** is to be given the worst job. And let's not forget that old Australian classic: **stone the crows!** (see entry).

croweater a person from South Australia. A derisive epithet dating back to the 1880s. See **cornstalk** for similar terms of derision for people from other states.

crust a living or livelihood. Common in the question *What do you do for a crust?*

cry Ruth to vomit. Also, **call for Ruth**.

Cunnamulla tune-up a prank tune-up in which spark plug leads are randomly swapped around. Not recommended by ten out of ten car mechanics.

cunning kick a secret pocket for hiding cash.

the Cup the Melbourne Cup horserace, held annually on the first Tuesday in November. The race which stops the entire country (except for wowsers). An Australian institution since Archer won it back in 1861. If you want to refer to a great length of time in Aussie lingo, you say **since Archer won the Cup**. The day on which the race is run is **Cup Day**, and the night before is **Cup Eve**, and the week in which it falls is **Cup Week**. And, come each

November, millions of Aussies are struck with **Cup fever**.

a cup of tea, a Bex, and a good lie down a method of relaxation once popular among Australian housewives. The phrase was originally a 1950s advertising line for the painkiller Bex. Unfortunately, at the time Bex was an APC, that is, a compound drug containing aspirin, phenacetin, and caffeine, which turned out to be highly addictive. The abuse of it led inexorably to renal disease. Eventually legislation was passed to outlaw the use of phenacetin in analgesic compounds and the abuse of the drug subsided. But, happily, the harmless and charming phrase has stayed with us.

cut-lunch commando derisive military slang for a member of the Australian Army Reserve. Since the 1950s.

cyberbludging wasting time at work using your employer's computer resources.

D

dack to pull someone's pants down; to pants someone. *I was dacked in front of everyone.*

Dad'n'Dave Aussie rhyming slang for 'shave'. Sometimes used to mean 'grave'. After the two comical characters created by Steele Rudd in the late 19th century.

dag 1. the Aussie species of the dweeb or nerd. This sense became common in the 1970s. Generally a direct insult, but of recent years there has been a movement for dags to 'reclaim' the word and be proud of their dagginess. This has had some partial success, so that calling someone a dag can now often be meant in an affectionate way. 2. a lump of excrement-matted wool on a sheep's rear.

daggy 1. uncool; conservative, lacking style and sophistication; dweebish, nerdy or geeky. Hence, **daggily**, in a daggy manner, and **dagginess**, the state of being daggy. 2. of sheep's wool, befouled with dags. Hence, of a person, dirty, slovenly and unkempt. Of clothing, old and worn-out.

daks pants. Generic use of a trademark. Sometimes spelt **dacks**. In use since the 1960s. Also appears in the compounds *chunder daks, dick daks, underdaks* and *trackie daks.*

Dalkeith tractor Perth slang, a derogatory term for a city-only 4WD that never sees off-road driving. Also called a **Dalkeith diesel**. See **Toorak tractor** for a host of synonyms.

Dapto briefcase in Wollongong, a cask of cheap wine. After Dapto, a small township in eastern NSW. Also called a **Bellambi handbag** or **goon box**.

Darwin rig the peculiar formal dress used in the Top End by men. Essentially there is no need for a jacket. After this you can replace the tie and collared shirt with an open-necked shirt, and long trousers can be replaced by shorts and long white socks. Thongs, stubbies and T-shirts are out. Also called **Territory rig**.

Darwin stubby a whopping bottle of beer, which at different times with different people, was anywhere from 40 to 80 fluid ounces (1.13 to 2.27 litres). Nowadays it is normally a 2.25 litre bottle and available widely in Darwin, especially for tourists.

dead fly biscuit a biscuit with dried fruit between two thin layers of sweet pastry; also called a **squashed fly biscuit** or a **fly cemetery**.

dead horse rhyming slang for 'tomato sauce'.

deadly 1. excellent, fantastic, cool, as in *She was a deadly spunk in an even deadlier skirt*. Originally a word of Aboriginal English, at least since the 1980s. Recently has made some crossover into the speech of white adolescents, especially in the NT. 2. also used as an adverb, as in *He sang deadly*.

deadly treadly classic Aussie slang for a bicycle. Generally, any bicycle could be a deadly treadly. Sometimes used to mean an excellent or fast bike. Other times used to mean a beat-up old bike. And other times used of one with a fixed wheel and no handbrakes, seen as unsafe. Has been around since the 1960s.

dead set 1. as an adverb, completely, totally, as in *I'm dead set against it*. 2. as an adjective, total, utter, as in *He's a dead set nong. No doubt about it*. 3. honestly! fair dinkum!

death adders in your pocket stingy or miserly.

the Deep North Queensland, or rather, Far North Queensland, viewed as a region of backwardness and intolerance. By analogy with America's Deep South.

der a mocking exclamation indicating faked and exaggerated stupidity or bewilderment. Equivalent to 'You idiot!' or 'As if!' Meant to represent the natural exclamation of a brainless person when attempting to think. Been around since the 1970s, principally among schoolkids.

dero a dismissive term for a derelict. Unsympathetic Aussie slang since the 1960s. Also, **derro**.

desk wallah a derisive term for a desk worker, especially a government official or bureaucrat. We also use the US term **desk jockey**.

dice to throw away, discard, reject. *The SP diced his sheets and tickets when he saw the copper approaching*. A nice bit of Aussie invention this one.

dick daks men's speedos. So called as they are daks that reveal the dick. Also known as

dick bathers. For a full set of synonyms see **sluggos**.

dick pointers the same as dick daks. Also called **dick pokers**. Politely abbreviated to **DPs**.

dick stickers yet another term for men's speedos. Chiefly used in NSW. In Qld the preferred term is **dick togs**, which is sometimes politely abbreviated to **DTs**. For a full set of synonyms see **sluggos**.

digger 1. in World War I, an Australian infantryman, used originally only of the lower ranks, not the officers. The term came about partly because the soldiers were required to dig trenches. Later became generalised to refer to any Anzac, no matter what the rank, and thence, in World War II and later conflicts, any Australian soldier. A term of great respect and pride. 2. a form of friendly address among men. Equivalent to *cobber* or *mate*. Now mostly used only when addressing elderly men. Both senses have an almost identical existence in New Zealand English.

digger hat an Australian Army slouch hat.

dill a fool; an incompetent; an absolute nong. Sometimes elaborated to **dill brain** or **dill pot**. Been around since the 1940s. In origin a backformation from **dilly**.

dilly bag a small traditional, hand-woven bag used by Aborigines. From the Aboriginal language Yagara, from the Brisbane region. Hence, applied to a toiletries bag, or to any small bag for various commodities.

dingbats 1. the delusions brought on by the DTs. 2. hence, as an adjective, crazy. *He's gone dingbats*.

ding-dong 1. of a fight, strenuously contested. A good fight is described as a *ding-dong go*. 2. powerful. *I've got a ding-dong headache*.

dingo 1. a no-good, pathetic coward. Aussie slang since the 1860s. After the native Australian dog, universally detested by early European settlers, and still held in great disrespect by many. 2. as a verb, to act in a cowardly manner; to back out ignominiously; to shirk or evade. 3. to **turn dingo** on someone is to betray them.

dingo's breakfast a piss and a good look round; that is, no breakfast at all. Also called a **bushman's breakfast**.

dink 1. to carry a second person on a horse, bicycle or motorcycle. Hence, such a ride, *I gave her a dink home*. Aussie slang since the 1930s. Used all over, but especially common in Vic, WA, ACT and Tas. There is a host of regional slang terms for this practice. There are three base words, **bar** (referring to the top metal bar of the bicycle frame), **dink** (perhaps from the British dialect word *dink* 'to dandle a baby') and the more obvious **double**. In Qld and NSW we find **bar** and **barie**. 'Bar' is especially common in south coast Qld and north coast NSW, and 'barie' is restricted to NSW only. Also especially common in Qld and NSW is the term **double**, which can be colloquially shortened to **dub**, or suffixed with *-er* to form **doubler**, which is also common in the ACT. Dink has provided us also with **dinky**, which is especially common in WA and SA. A combination of two of the base words, has given us **double-dink** (especially WA, Victoria and Tasmania) and **dinky-double** (chiefly NSW and ACT). South Australia has gone out on its own with the term **donkey**. Which is partly from the name of the animal and partly an alteration of *dinky*. **2.** one of a couple, married or unmarried, who have separate incomes and no children. An acronym from *Double Income, No Kids*. One of the few survivors of the rash of acronyms for various sociological types during the 1980s. **3.** an abbreviation of **dinkum**. *Are you dink?*

dinkum **1.** genuine. As in, *Are you dinkum about that?* or *She was a dinkum Queenslander all right*. It appears earliest in the phrase *fair dinkum* (1890 in Australia, but 1881 in Britain), and not as a separate word until 1905. Comes from the British dialects of Derbyshire and Lincolnshire, where it meant 'work', or 'a due share of work'. So if you did your fair dinkum, it meant you did your fair share of the work. The claim that the word was brought to Australia by Chinese miners in the gold rush era (from Cantonese *din kum* 'real gold') cannot be true, unless there was a secret population of Chinese goldminers in the south of England that no-one knows about. Seems a bit unlikely. Altered variously to **dink**, **dinks** and **dinky-di**. **2.** used as an adverb, really, genuinely. As in, *He's me mate, dinkum he is!*

dinkum Aussie a genuine Australian, exhibiting all those aspects of the Australian character that we like to believe Australians have, like honesty, courage, laconic sense of humour, willingness to work hard, and so on.

dinky-di a slangier version of **dinkum**. Used since the 1910s. *He's a dinky-di Aussie.*

dip out 1. to opt out or not join in. *'Another beer, mate?' 'Sorry, I'll have to dip out.'* **2.** to miss out on an opportunity. *I tried waiting around for an autograph, but dipped out.* Hence, to fail. *Hewitt dipped out in the first round.*

dip your lid to lift your hat as a mark of respect. Hence, metaphorically, to show admiration. Commonly used in the ungrammatical phrase *I dips me lid*, in allusion to C.J. Dennis' Sentimental Bloke who dips his lid upon first meeting his lady love Doreen.

the Dirty Acre a 3/4 acre block in the middle of the Golden Mile near Kalgoorlie. It was sold for 12 bottles of champagne in the 1890s by Tom Brookman and Sam Pearce (the discoverers of the Golden Mile). The small block was quickly covered with 5 hotels, a brewery and numerous other shops. Miners used to tunnel up into the cellars of the hotels to sell stolen gold over the bar. The 'Sunday Sesh' at the Block was a riotous affair right up to the early 1990s when the last hotel was demolished to make way for mining operations.

the Dirty Half Mile that strip of the Sydney suburb of Kings Cross renowned for prostitution and vice. So called since the 1930s.

divvy 1. services slang, an infantry division. Used by Aussies since World War I. **2.** in gambling slang, a dividend or payout; a collect. **3.** a portion of profits, especially when illegally gained. Hence, to **divvy up**, to share out.

divvy van a police van for the conveyance of those in custody. Used all over Australia, but especially common in Victoria. Sometimes spelt **divi-van**.

do 1. a festivity or party. *We're having a big do next week.* **2.** to injure. *He did his ankle jumping from a train.* **3.** to spend all your money. *He did his dough at the races.* Great Australian pastime since the 1890s. **4.** of a person, to be admirable. Used as a compliment or statement of praise. As in *You'll do, mate*, or, *How about that fullback? He'll do me!*

do a Melba to make a habit of returning from retirement, in a number of 'farewell' performances. Alluding to the famous opera singer Dame Nellie *Melba*.

dob 1. to tell on someone; to report someone to the

authorities. A cardinal sin in Australia. *I'll tell you if you promise not to dob.* You can dob *on* someone, or dob them *in*. Been around since the 1950s. If you **dob someone in**, you nominate them for an unpleasant task. **2.** in Aussie slang, to **dob in** also has another meaning, namely, to contribute funds to a collection. This also dates back to the 1950s.

dobber an informer or telltale. A term of high opprobrium in Australia. An older variant was **dobber-in**, but this is not heard much any more. Both terms date back to the 1950s.

doctor a cool, southerly sea breeze that blows after a hot day. Also called the **Albany doctor**, **Esperance doctor** or **Fremantle doctor**, depending upon where you are in WA.

dodgy liable to be dishonest, suspect, as in a *dodgy salesman*, or a *dodgy call*. Also means not stable or reliable. *Those foundations look a bit dodgy. He's got a dodgy hamstring.* Laconically shortened to **dodge**. *Man, that Picasso you bought looks a bit dodge.* Also extended to **dodge-a-rama**.

Dodgy Brothers a group or company that is known to be, or acts, in a dodgy or underhanded manner. From the name of a comedy act in the 1980s TV series *Australia – You're Standing In It*.

doer a hard and keen worker; one who succeeds through hard, honest work. *He was a real little doer.* A term of respect. The opposite of a bludger. Has been part of Australian culture since at least the 1900s. A particularly hard worker was known as a **hard doer**.

dog **1.** in underworld slang, an informer. Hence, to **turn dog**, to betray someone to the authorities. **2.** a prison warder or other prison authority.

dog and bone Aussie rhyming slang for 'telephone'.

dog's eye Aussie rhyming slang for 'meat pie'. So called since the 1950s. Hence a **dog's eye and dead horse** is a pie and sauce. Also known as a **bleeding dog's eye**.

dog squad undercover police.

dole bludger a derisive term for an unemployed person living off social security payments without making proper attempts to find a job. The term first came to prominence in the 1970s. An earlier term was **doley**, which had been in use since the 1950s.

do like a dinner to vanquish. Aussie slang since the 1840s.

the Don Sir Donald Bradman, Australia's greatest batsman, Test captain 1936–48.

dong to hit or punch. *I donged him on the head.* Hence, a heavy blow. The Aussie love of stoushing has produced this little beauty, dating back to the 1910s.

donga 1. the bush or outback. *He's been out in the donga too long.* 2. a makeshift or temporary dwelling; hence, a demountable, especially in a mining area.

donkey-lick to defeat with ease. Commonly used in horseracing. Aussie slang since the 1890s.

don't come the raw prawn Don't try to deceive me. *Don't come the raw prawn with me! How can you say you can't stand 'em when you've never even touched one!* A 'prawn' is a fool, and a 'raw prawn' is a naive fool. Originally Australian military slang from World War II. A jocular variant of this phrase is **don't come the uncooked crustacean**.

doover a doodad or thingummyjig. Also expanded to **dooverlackie**. Originally Australian military slang of World War II. A general utility term which could mean a manoeuvre, an exercise, a thing, a soldier, etc. Was commonly used to refer to a dugout or shelter. Said by some to be from *do for*, as in the phrase *that will do for now*. Others prefer a Yiddish origin.

do the Harry to run away or leave promptly; make oneself scarce. In full **do the Harold Holt**, rhyming slang for 'bolt'. Referring to our erstwhile Prime Minister who disappeared while swimming without so much as saying hooroo.

Double Bay tractor Sydney slang, a derogatory term for a city-only 4WD that never sees off-road driving. Also called a **Double Bay shopping trolley**. See **Toorak tractor** for a host of synonyms.

down the gurgler ruined; irretrievably lost or destroyed. The home-grown Aussie version of the usual 'down the drain' or 'down the plughole'. Been around since the 1970s.

Down Under Australia. Also used of New Zealand, and of Australia and NZ together. Originally from the British point of view – as though they were on top. Despite this slightly negative perspective the term has been embraced by us Antipodeans and has been in use since the 1880s.

drag the chain to lag behind. A metaphor from the chain gangs of convict days, but not recorded from that era, first making its appearance in the 1910s, where it seemed originally to be a phrase used in the shearing sheds for the slowest shearer.

drink with the flies to drink alone when at a pub. Since 1910s.

drive the porcelain bus to vomit into a toilet bowl.

drongo a slow-witted or stupid person; a fool. A great Australian insult. Originally it was an RAAF term for a raw recruit, and first appears in the early 1940s. From *Drongo*, the name of a racehorse in the early 1920s which was famed for its poor form and used as a character in the political cartoons of Sammy Wells appearing in the *Melbourne Herald*. Some have suggested that it refers to the spangled drongo, a tropical bird of northeast Australia, but there doesn't appear to be any obvious connection.

drop bear a vicious breed of koala that supposedly leaps upon unsuspecting tourists and attacks with unmitigated fury. A tale told to frighten unwary foreigners since at least the 1960s.

drop the kids off at the pool to go to the toilet for number twos.

drunk as Chloe extremely drunk. The origin of this phrase is a mystery. It is not derived from the famous painting of *Chloe* in Young and Jackson's Hotel, Melbourne, as the expression appeared in Britain in the 1820s and the painting was not around till 1875. Apart from Chloe, it is common in Oz to be **drunk as a lord**, **drunk as a skunk**, **drunk as a pissant**, **drunk as a tick**, and even **drunk as Larry Dooley**, whoever he was.

dry as a dead dingo's donger completely dry; parched; badly in need of a life-giving beer.

dubbo in NSW, a fool or imbecile. From *Dubbo*, a town in rural NSW, viewed as a source of country bumpkins. Has been around since the 1970s.

duck's disease shortness of stature.

duck's guts the very best: *That meal was the duck's guts!* Also heard as the **duck's nuts**.

duckshove 1. to evade a responsibility. 2. to illegally move your hand over the line when shooting in a game of marbles. See **fanannywhacking** for a full set of synonyms.

dud 1. a failure of a person; a loser. *That guy is an absolute dud.* 2. to swindle or cheat. *I suddenly realised I had been dudded.*

duds trousers; pants. *Hang on while I get me duds on.* Aussie slang since the 1920s. Formerly used to refer to clothes in general.

duff 1. old Aussie slang meaning to steal cattle. 2. to mess up or fluff – the sort of thing a silly duffer does. *It was an easy putt, but he's duffed it.* 3. If a woman is **up the duff**, then she is pregnant. This is probably from old slang *duff* = pudding, as in 'in the pudding club'.

dumper a wave which, in shallow water, instead of breaking evenly from the top, crashes violently down, throwing swimmers or surfers to the bottom. Picked up by American surfers and now used in the US.

dunny 1. (originally) an outside toilet, found in unsewered areas, usually at some distance from the house it serves and consisting of a small shed furnished with a lavatory seat placed over a sanitary can or pit. Iconic Australiana. First recorded in the 1930s, it is a shortening of *dunniken*, which had been around since the 1840s, but has now completely died out, being last seen in the 1960s. However, toilet blocks, say at school, or in a caravan park, are still known as **the dunnies**. In schoolyards, 'behind the dunnies' is a common place for all sorts of activities not approved of by the teaching staff, such as cigarette smoking, fighting, and amorous liaisons. 2. a sanitary can or toilet bowl. *Damn it, I dropped my watch in the dunny.* 3. the toilet or bathroom. 4. the ubiquity of the dunny in Australia has led to it being immortalised in a number of slang phrases. To be **all alone like a country dunny** is to be completely alone or isolated. A highly-sexed woman is said to **bang like a dunny door in a gale** – absolutely charming metaphor that one. Someone who is brainless **couldn't train a choko vine to grow up a dunny wall**, and something useless is described as being **as useful as a glass door on a dunny**. If your luck is out you can exclaim **If it was raining palaces I'd be hit on the head by the dunny door**. Finally, if someone's luck is in, and you wish that it would change for the worse, you may cry **I hope your chooks turn into emus and kick your dunny down!**

dunny budgie a blowfly.

dunny can in the days before sewerage, a removable can forming the receptacle of the toilet. The unsavoury job of emptying these cans was the occupation of the **dunny man**. A detailed account of the dunny man's art is to be found in Frank Hardy's novel *The Outcasts of Foolgarah* – if you're interested.

dunny cart a horse-drawn cart used by the dunny man, formerly a feature of the Australian landscape.

dunny documents toilet paper.

durry Aussie slang for a cigarette. Been around since the 1940s. The origin is a bit of a mystery. Some claimed it to be from Bull *Dur*ham, a brand of tobacco, but this seems a little far-fetched. Another theory is that it is from *dhurrie*, a type of cotton mat, referring to the shape when rolled up. Who knows?

dust devil a miniature whirlwind that picks up dust and rubbish, common in the outback.

E

Eastern Suburbs Holden a Sydney slang term for a Mercedes-Benz.

easybeat a person who is easily beaten. In the plural it refers to a team you can wipe the floor with who are probably the cellar dwellers. Of course, this term owes its origin to the great 1960s Oz band *The Easybeats*.

echo in SA, a small beer bottle that was able to be returned for a refund and was then washed and re-used. Nowadays glass bottles are recycled, but the term is still in use.

eh a tag used at the end of a statement generally inviting assent, as in *Wasn't that lucky, eh?* or *Great fun, eh?* In Queensland (and New Zealand), used repetitiously at the end of virtually every statement, without any sense of it being a question. *I was goin' down the shops, eh. And I ran into Johnno, eh. Hadn't seen him for weeks, eh.*

the Ekka 1. the Brisbane Exhibition showground. 2. the Royal Queensland Show.

elastics a girls' schoolyard game in which a long loop of elastic is held, usually between two children, and a set of various trick manoeuvres with the legs is performed by a third. After the completion of a set without mistakes the elastic is moved up higher thus increasing the difficulty. Also called **elastic skippy**.

Elvis Presley among car salesmen, a car with many dents in the body and scratches in the duco. That is, it has had many hits.

Emerald City a nickname for Sydney – so called from its sunny splendour and jewel-like magnificence, its glorious harbour and stunning architecture, equal to the fabled city that was home to the Wizard of Oz.

Emma Chisit the question 'How much is it?' as rendered in Strine. The beginning point and probably the most famous piece of Strine ever. First heard (or rather, misheard) in the 1960s. If you don't know what

Strine is, you can look it up at the entry for **Strine**.

emu-bob to bend down to pick up things, as timber, roots, or the like, in order to clear an area. Hence, **emu-bobber**, a person doing this. Specifically, a person who stacks up sticks after a burning-off job. Also, at the racecourse, a fossicker after discarded betting tickets.

emu parade originally, a military parade to clean an area of litter. Dating back to World War II. Hence, any similar collection of people collecting litter or other unwanted material from an area. Commonly schoolkids are seconded for this job. Also, a line of police combing an area for forensic evidence. It can also be called an **emu bob**, an **emu patrol**, or an **emu walk**, and in WA, an **emu stalk**.

esky a portable icebox. Quintessential item of Australian living. A trademark term, from *eskimo*, but used generically.

esky lid a disparaging term used by surfies for a bodyboard. Hence, a bodyboarder is called an **esky lidder**.

Esperance doctor See **doctor**.

ex-govie in the ACT, a house built by the Commonwealth Government but now privately owned.

exy expensive. *The suit looks pretty exy*. Also spelt **exxy**.

F

face like a ... someone with an ugly face is said to have a **face like a smashed crab**. Other sad cases include a **face like the northbound end of a southbound cow**, and a **face like a half-eaten pastie**. Compare **head like a ...**.

fair cop 1. a just punishment or outcome. 2. an unequivocal busting of someone red-handed.

fair crack of the whip! an appeal for fairness.

fair dinkum 1. true or genuine; real, as opposed to phoney. *It's the fair dinkum article all right*. One of the best-known, best-loved and most enduring of all Australian slang phrases. Found in Oz since the 1890s. Comes from north Lincolnshire dialect of England (recorded in 1881), where it meant 'fair play'. For more info on the origin, see **dinkum**. 2. fair and equitable. *It was the only fair dinkum raffle run in the pub's history*. 3. in earnest. As in *Are you fair dinkum?* meaning 'Are you serious?' 4. showing typical Australian honesty, guts, directness and the like. *They were all fair dinkum blokes and sheilas*. 5. well and truly. *He was fair dinkum pissing himself laughing*. 6. really, honestly. As in, *It's true, mate, fair dinkum*. In this sense can be shortened to **fair dink** or **fair dinks**.

fair go a fair or reasonable opportunity; just treatment. As in *He never had a fair go*. This phrase has been around since the 1900s. Giving people a fair go is a quintessential aspect of the national character. Hence used as an appeal for fairness or reason. Equivalent to 'Be fair!' *Fair go, mate!*

fair suck of the sauce bottle! Be fair! Classic Australiana. Very 70s. Also heard as **fair suck of the sav**, and even **fair suck of the Siberian sandshoe!** Or laconically shortened to the simple **fair suck!**

fairy floss the peculiar Australian moniker for the pink spun sugar you get at fetes and the like. What the Poms call candy floss, and the Yanks call cotton candy.

falcon in Rugby League, originally being hit in the face with the ball, but now, any accidental headbutt. So called in honour of a famous incident involving the face of Mario Fenech, nicknamed 'the Maltese Falcon', or simply, 'the Falcon', because of his Maltese background.

fanannywhacking the action of illegally moving your hand over the line when shooting in a game of marbles. Someone who commits this crime is known by the opprobrious title of **fanannywhacker**. Australian schoolkids have been quite inventive when it comes to this crime, which is known around the country by the names **cribs**, **cribbing**, **duckshoving**, **fnudging** (or **phernudging**), **fudging**, and **lagging**.

fang 1. to drive at great speed; to hoon. Aussie slang since the 1960s. Supposedly in honour of the famous Argentinian F1 racing driver Juan Fangio. Hence, a speedy drive or hoon. *I'm going for a fang around the block*. **2.** a tooth. Hence, a bite, as in *I gave it an exploratory fang*. To be **good on the fang** is to be a hearty eater, or a **fang artist**. To **go the fang** on something, or to **fang down** on it, is to hoe into it. As a verb, to **fang** is to crave food, as in *I'm fanging for a steak*, or to eat voraciously, as in *She sat there fanging away for all she was worth*. **3.** to **put the fangs into** someone is to attempt to borrow from them. To **fang** then can also be used as a verb, as in *I fanged him for a couple of bucks*.

fang carpenter a dentist. Also called a **fang farrier**.

Farmer Giles Aussie rhyming slang for 'piles', as in haemorrhoids. Dates back to the 1960s.

farnarkling activity which creates an appearance of productivity but which has no substance to it. Coined by comedian John Clarke for a fictitious team sport for which he acted as sports commentator in the 1980s television series *The Gillies Report*.

feature with to have sexual intercourse with. Aussie slang dating from the 1960s – a favourite expression of the inimitable Bazza McKenzie.

feed the fishes to be seasick; occasionally used to refer to drowning.

feral 1. a type of hippie environmentalist. There are the real ferals who live in the bush, fight loggers and generally try to make a difference, and then there are the faux inner-city ferals who look the part

ferret

with their dreads and rainbow-coloured clothing, but live with as many of the mod cons as they so desire. **2.** a westie, bevan or bogan. **3.** among teenagers, disgusting or gross. **4.** wild or unrestrained in behaviour. *The kids have gone feral.*

ferret 1. in cricket, a player at the tail-end of the batting order. So called since they follow the *bunnies* or *rabbits* in. **2.** the penis, in such Bazza McKenzie inspired phrases as **give the ferret a run**, **exercise the ferret**, and **run the ferret up the drainpipe**, which mean to engage in sexual intercourse or to urinate.

festy 1. dirty; grubby; unclean and smelly. **2.** extremely bad; awful; dreadful.

few in Australia if you are going to 'have a few' it has only one meaning – namely, a few ice-cold beers.

fifty-fifty 1. a glass of beer, half old and half new. Also, called simply **fifty**. *I'll have a glass of fifty, love.* **2.** a dance, usually held in a country or suburban hall, at which the dancing and music is half old-time and half modern.

fire o'clock among firefighters, the time in the afternoon when school finishes in summer, after which kids light fires.

firie a firefighter. Also spelt **firee** or **fire-ie**.

First Fleeter a person whose lineage can be traced back to the occupants of the First Fleet in 1788. A cause for great pride in Australia since as early as 1826.

fish frighteners speedos. For a full set of synonyms see **sluggos**.

fit as a mallee bull supremely fit and healthy.

five o'clock wave a fictitious wave passing down the Murrumbidgee River through Wagga Wagga each day, supposedly created by the release of water from an upriver dam. A tale told to unwary visitors. *If you get your surfboard and hurry down to Wagga Beach you can catch the five o'clock wave.*

flaming fury a toilet constructed over a pit, the contents of which are periodically doused with oil and burnt.

flannie a flannelette shirt with a coloured checked pattern. The emblematic dress of westies, bevans and bogans. Also called a **flanno**. One of the few words which has both an *-ie* and an *-o* form.

flash as a rat with a gold tooth extremely showy or ostentatious.

flash for cash a police speed camera or radar trap.

flash language the specialised jargon of the criminal class spoken in colonial times. Also called **the flash**. This term originated in England in the 18th century and was brought to Australia by transported convicts. There are quite a number of flash terms still forming part of modern Australian slang, including **conk, gammon** and **new chum** (see those entries for more information).

flat chat at full speed. *He drove flat chat down the road.* Also occasionally in the form **flat bickie** or **flat strap**.

fleas and itches Aussie rhyming slang for 'the pictures', that is, the cinema.

floater 1. a meat pie served in pea soup. Recorded since 1915. An Aussie culinary treat. 2. in prison, an item, such as a book or magazine, that is kept illegally by prisoners and smuggled from cell to cell. 3. in wharfie slang, a worker not attached to a gang. 4. a dead person found floating in the ocean, a river, or the like. 5. a floating piece of excrement in a toilet – one that won't flush.

flog 1. to steal. 2. to sell, especially something that you have obtained illegally.

flogger a short stick with a bunch of crepe paper streamers in team colours attached, used in barracking in Aussie Rules.

floordrobe a clothing system which entails the floor littered with discarded clothes. More like a **pack of poo tickets** than a wardrobe.

flybog jam. Because it will bog flies if they land in it.

fly cemetery a biscuit with dried fruit sandwiched between two thin layers of sweet biscuit. Also called a **fly pie**.

flying cane toad a disparaging name for the much hated Indian myna, a feral bird introduced into Australia in the 1860s and now common around large cities and cane-growing areas along the eastern coast. In reality, they are nowhere near as bad as cane toads. Also known as the **garbage bird**.

fnudge to illegally move your hand over the line when shooting in a game of marbles. *Hey – no fnudging!* Also spelt **phernudge**. See **fanannywhacking** for a full set of synonyms.

footbrawl a derogatory term for football – either Aussie Rules or the two Rugby codes, but not soccer, which is known as **catch and kiss**.

footy **1.** football. Aussie slang since the 1900s. In WA, SA, Vic and Tas this, of course, means Aussie Rules. Whereas in NSW and Qld it pretty much means Rugby League or Union. In Britain it means soccer. **2.** a football. *Who kicked the footy over the fence?*

fourby **1.** a piece of four-by-two. A dimension of timber Australians have taken to their hearts. *I got whacked on the scone with a great lump of fourby.* **2.** a four-wheel-drive.

franger **1.** Aussie slang for a condom. Since the 1970s. **2.** a sausage. Also **frang**.

freeballing of a man, wearing no underdaks under the daks. Also known as **free snaking it**.

Fremantle doctor See **doctor**.

freshie a freshwater crocodile.

friend of Dorothy a homosexual man. From Dorothy in *The Wizard of Oz*, played by Judy Garland, a gay icon.

frostie an ice-cold beer. Sometimes called a **frosty chop**.

full completely intoxicated; pissed as a newt. This word has given rise to numerous similes, such as **full as a boot** or **full as a goog** which can mean (a) drunk, (b) satiated after a meal, or (c) overcrowded. Apart from boots and googs, you can be **full as a bull, a bull's bum, a butcher's pup, an egg, a family jerry** or **po, a Catholic school, a State school, a State school hat rack, a fart, a tick, a Pommy's complaint box,** or **a fat lady's sock** (or **bra/knickers/undies,** etc.).

full up to dolly's wax satiated after a fine meal; replete with food; stonkered. *I couldn't eat another crumb, I'm full up to dolly's wax.* Referring to an old type of child's doll which had a cloth body and a head made of wax. You can also be **full up to pussy's bow** or **ribbon**.

furphy a rumour. From the name of a brand of water cart manufactured by J. Furphy and Sons, which, during World War I, were natural centres of gossip.

fuzzy wuzzy angels during World War II, a term used for the native Papua New Guineans who gave great assistance to Australian soldiers.

G

galah a fool. *Get out of it, you great bloody galah.* Someone acting the fool is described as **mad as a gumtree full of galahs**.

galah session a time set aside for the people of isolated outback areas to converse with one another by radio.

game as Ned Kelly imbued with the fighting spirit of Australia's national hero; plucky; resolute. You can also be as **game as Phar Lap**, Australia's other great national hero.

gammon 1. to lie or tell fibs; to pretend or kid; to tease. *I'm just gammoning.* Originally slang used by the criminal class, first recorded back in 1812. This word has survived over the years largely as a part of Aboriginal English, from where it has now been re-adopted into the speech of white people, especially in areas where they have contact with Aboriginal communities (as northern Australia). 2. as a noun, a lie or fib; nonsense or rubbish; a fake; something no good. *I don't believe you. That's gammon!* Also used as an exclamation of disbelief.

garbo a garbage collector. Also refers to a garbage bin. *Chuck it in the garbo.*

garbologist a garbage collector.

gazunder 1. a chamber-pot. It 'goes under' the bed. 2. in cricket, a mullygrubber.

G'day the ubiquitous friendly Australian greeting. Recorded in this abbreviated form since the 1900s. *G'day mate, how're you goin'?* Sometimes written out in full as **good day**, but it is always pronounced as 'G'day'. Occasionally written as **gidday**. When pronounced as two separate words, this was formerly used as a parting comment, generally when the person leaving was annoyed. *Good day to you sir!* This old-fashioned use is occasionally still used nowadays, but only in a joking way.

the Gee a nickname for the Melbourne Cricket Ground or MCG.

gee up to excite or stir up, as in *Her act really geed the audience* *up*. Hence, as a noun, an instance of stirring up enthusiasm, raising spirits or the like. *The big crowd gave the players a much needed gee up.*

gent among fishos, a maggot used for bait. Way back in the 16th century anglers used to call maggots *gentles*, from an old meaning of the word *gentle* 'soft to the touch'.

Germaine Greer Aussie rhyming slang for a 'beer'. Dates from the 1980s.

get a black dog up you! meaning 'Get stuffed!' Actually, the dog doesn't necessarily have to be black as you can say 'Get a dog up ya!'

get a guernsey originally, to be selected for a football team. Hence, to be selected for any team, or for anything.

giggle hat the standard Army issue hat for jungle wear. Floppy things made from cotton twill. Known officially as 'hats utility, jungle green'. Also called **hats ridiculous** or simply **bush hats**.

giggle house an asylum for the insane. Digger slang from World War I. Also called a **giggle factory**.

ging (pronounced with an initial hard 'g') a child's catapult or slingshot. Perhaps imitative of the sound made when fired. Aussie slang since the 1930s. Now chiefly used in WA and Qld.

ginger 1. the backside or bum. *I gave him a swift kick up the ginger*. From **ginger ale**, rhyming slang for 'tail'. If someone is **on your ginger**, then they are chasing you. If you are in a car, then the bastard is tailgating you. 2. of a prostitute or their accomplice, to thieve from a client's clothing.

ginger beer Aussie rhyming slang for 'engineer', especially an engineer in the armed forces. Dates back to the 1940s.

give the game away to abandon whatever it is you're doing.

go 1. an attempt. *I'll give anything a go*. Hence the great Aussie barracking cry: *Have a go ya mug!* 2. a fight. *When the rival fans met in the pub, boy, then you'd see some goes*. Commonly found in that great Aussie challenge to fisticuffs, *Do you want a go, mate?* Hence, as a verb, to attack, as in *I was itching to go him*. 3. an opportunity fit for taking. *Here's a go!* A fair chance, as in *There's no chance of getting a go here*. 4. to say, as in *So I go to him, 'Shut your face!'* Used mostly by schoolkids, but also common in the speech of ethnic Australians. Kylie Mole of the hit 1980s TV show *The Comedy Company* was a past master at this idiom: *Mum went to me that Dino went to her to go to me that he isn't wif Amanda anymore.* **5.** to eat or drink with pleasure. *I could really go a beer right now.* **6.** a goanna. *You should have seen that go go!* A great example of the Aussie penchant for abbreviation.

goanna Aussie rhyming slang for 'pianner', that is, a piano. Dates back to World War I.

go for the doctor to go all out; to go as fast as you can. Also, to bet all your money on a race. In horseracing, it is the moment when the jockey gets the whip out and goes for broke.

the Golden Mile a gold-bearing reef lying between Kalgoorlie and Boulder in WA.

golly saliva and mucus collected in the mouth and spat out. Hence, as a verb, to spit.

gone to Gowings NSW slang, absolutely gone; gone in all respects. Originally an advertising slogan from the 1940s for Sydney department store *Gowing* Bros Ltd. The ad campaign consisted of witty cartoons of someone making a hasty departure with the explanation that they had 'Gone to Gowings'. When notorious criminal Darcy Dugan escaped from jail in the late 1940s he scrawled on the cell wall 'Gone to Gowings'. Specifically the expression can mean destitute, drunk, hungover, losing a race or game dismally, insane, or merely, and in the original sense, departed in great haste. Sadly, the well-known Sydney retail store closed its doors early in 2006, after 138 years of business – so now Gowings is finally gone.

the Gong the city of Wollongong, just south of Sydney.

gonk a kid's catapult or slingshot. A word from the north coast of NSW. See **slingshot** for synonyms.

gooby a mass of nasal mucus ejected from the mouth. Also called a **golly**, or in Victoria, a **gorby**.

good-bye muscles the flabby triceps of an overweight or matronly woman.

good guts useful information; the good oil; the drum. World War II Aussie slang.

good-oh all right, okay. *Everything was good-oh.* Commonly used as an exclamation.

the good oil reliable information; the lowdown; the drum. Also called the **dinkum oil**, or simply, **the oil**.

good on you! Well done! Bravo! Commonly heard as **good onya**, or shortened simply to **onya!** In the plural, it is, of course, **good onyas!**

good sort a spunky woman. Aussie blokes have been referring to delectable sheilas as good sorts since at least the 1940s. In recent years the term has been adopted by women to refer to spunky men.

good trot a run of good luck. Aussie slang from at least the 1940s.

good wicket an advantageous position. *He's on a good wicket*.

go off 1. of a party or similar event, to be thrilling. *The dance floor was really going off*, or *It was a great night, it really went off*. If it really goes off, then it is said to **go off like a frog in a sock**. 2. of the surf, to produce excellent waves. 3. of an illegal establishment, to be raided by police. Aussie underworld slang dating from the 1940s. Hence, to be arrested by the police. 4. of a racehorse, to make a proper run in a race after being previously held back to give an impression of poor form in order to obtain good odds.

goom methylated spirits drunk by alcoholics. First recorded in the 1960s, and perhaps from an Aboriginal language. Hence a **goomie** is a person addicted to methylated spirits.

goon 1. originally, a flagon of wine. First appears in the 1980s. Some have suggested that it is from *flagoon*, a jocular pronunciation of *flagon*. They might be right. 2. cheap cask wine; plonk. This meaning first appears in the 1990s. Also called **goonie**. An aficionado of such booze is known as a **goon monkey**.

goon bag the silver bladder of wine inside a wine cask. Also called a **goonie bag** or **goon sack**. **Goon bag soccer** is a type of drunken soccer played with an inflated silver bladder from a wine cask – typically has plenty of 'diving' but no shonky refs to hand out bodgie penalties.

goon box a cask of cheap wine. Also called a **gooner**.

goon juice a drink made from soft drink mixed with cask wine.

goon-of-fortune a backyard party at which the bladders of wine casks are hung from a Hills hoist and accessed by spinning the hoist around – guests have to fill their glass from whichever goon sack fate chooses for them. Also called **goonie party**.

gorby a chiefly Victorian word for a mass of nasal mucus ejected from the mouth. Elsewhere called a **gooby** or **golly**.

govie in the ACT, a government-funded residence, usually offering low-cost accommodation. Also spelt **guvvie**.

gravel rash **1.** what you get from being a crawler. *He's covered in gravel rash from crawling to the boss.* In use since World War I. **2.** See **pash rash**.

great Australian adjective the word *bloody* used as an intensifier; once ubiquitous in Australian colloquial speech. So called since the 1890s.

green can a can of Victoria Bitter beer. As opposed to a **blue**, **red**, **white** or **yellow can** (see entries).

green giant a plastic $100 note.

gremmie a derogatory term for a young inexperienced surfer.

gremmie

From **gremlin**, in the same sense. Also called a **grommet**.

grey ghost See **brown bomber**.

grey nomad an older person, often retired, who travels around the country in a caravan or motorhome.

grey nurse an old paper $100 note. From its colour. Now replaced by the **green giant**.

grommet a derogatory term for a young inexperienced surfer. Also shortened to **grom** or **grommie**. Aussie slang at least since the 1980s. Now also used by snowboarders for novice snowboarders. Also called a **gremmie**.

groper a West Australian. A derogatory term from as far back as the 1890s. A shortening of **sandgroper**. Hence, **Groperland** is Western Australia. See **cornstalk** for similar terms of derision for people from other states.

grouse Aussie slang for very good. *We had a grouse time, but it's back to work now*. Been around since the 1920s, and still very much in favour. Origin unknown. Can also be used as a noun, as in *My new car is the grouse*.

grouter to **come in on the grouter** is to arrive after the work's finished, either through luck or contrivance. Laying the grout is the last job to get done when tiling. Hence, to be lucky, to have things fall your way; to take advantage of an opportune circumstance. Used in a disparaging way by those who haven't had the luck. *Have you noticed how the bludger always manages to come in on the grouter?*

grundies Aussie rhyming slang for 'undies'. Short for **Reg Grundies**.

gumi in the Riverina, a raft made predominantly of tyre inner tubes. There is a **gumi race** down the Murrumbidgee River held annually. Interestingly, the word *gumi* is pidgin English for rubber.

gumsucker a disparaging appellation for a person from Victoria dating from the 1840s. This originally referred to the habit of chewing on the gum exuded from wattle trees. See **cornstalk** for similar terms of derision for people from other states.

gumtree the beautiful Australian eucalypt, so named from its gummy sap. A term first used by James Cook in 1770. Used in some slang expressions, namely **up a gumtree**, in all sorts of strife, and **mad as a gumtree full of galahs**, stark raving bonkers.

gumtree mail a system of letter delivery in remote bush areas, whereby the sender finds a cleft stick lying around underneath a gumtree, places a letter in it and waits for a passing train. The driver or guard snatches up the letter as the train passes by, and hence it finds its way into the mailbag.

gun **1.** a champion shearer. Aussie slang since the 1890s. Hence a champion at any endeavour. **2.** a large surfboat for riding big waves. **3.** to rev an engine; hence, to drive at great speed.

guts **1.** essential information. *We need to get to the guts of the matter.* Digger slang from World War I. Hence, the **good guts** is useful info, the good oil, the drum. **2.** to **drop your guts** is to fart.

H

had the dick ruined, busted, worn out, wrecked, no good. Also found in the forms **had the rod**, **had the sword** and **had the stick**, and euphemised to **had the Richard**, where Richard means Dick.

hairy goat a poor racehorse. If a racehorse **runs like a hairy goat**, then it won't be winning any races.

hammer 1. heroin. Short for *hammer and tack*, Aussie rhyming slang for 'smack'. 2. also rhyming slang for 'back'. Thus if someone is **on your hammer**, then they are following you closely, or, when in a car, tailgating you. 3. to drive at speed. *We were hammering up the freeway.*

handbag an attractive male used by a woman as a showpiece when going out to social functions. Aussie woman's slang since the 1960s.

handbrake a man's wife or girlfriend viewed as an obstacle to enjoyment. *Davo's not coming to the footy, he's got his handbrake on tonight.*

happy as a bastard on Father's Day unhappy. There's nothing like Father's Day to remind the bastard of their fatherlessness. Classic Aussie saying since the 1950s.

happy as Larry extremely happy. Just who the gladsome Larry was, and how he could have been happy enough to become a byword for joy, is unknown.

happy little vegemite a person in a good mood. *Look at the happy little vegemites working away in there*. First appears in the 1980s in this slang sense, originating in the well-loved advertising jingle for the spread Vegemite which first filled Australian airwaves back in 1954.

hard yakka good, solid, back-breaking work. See the entry for **yakka** for more information.

Harold Holt Aussie rhyming slang for 'bolt', meaning flee. Referring to the former Australian PM who disappeared while swimming in the ocean. Also simply shortened to

Harold or **Harry**. Occasionally used as a rhyme for 'salt'.

have a shot at to attack verbally. *He had a shot at me about me swearing.* Aussie slang since the 1820s.

have it off to have sex. Unromantic Aussie sexual slang since at least the 1960s.

have tickets on yourself to have an inflated view of yourself.

Hay, Hell and Booligal hot and uncomfortable places; places to be avoided. From the Banjo Paterson poem by this name. Hay and Booligal are towns on the plains of inland NSW.

headless chicken to **run around like a headless chicken** is to act without rhyme or reason. A classic Australianism since the 1950s. Of course, even more Australian is to use the variant **headless chook**.

head like a ... Someone with an ugly head is said to have a **head like a half-sucked mango**. Even worse is to have a **head like a half-sucked mango and a body like a burst sausage**. Other sad cases include a **head like a half-sucked cheezel**, or a **head like a dropped meat-pie**. Still more include a **head like a racing tadpole**, a **head like a revolving mallee root**, a **head like a Turkish trotting duck**, and a **head like a busted sofa**. Man, there are some ugly heads out there! Compare **face like a ....**

heifer paddock a girl's school.

hide effrontery or impudence. Unbeknown to most people, this is an Australian original, dating back to the 1900s. To have **more hide than Jessie** is to be supremely impudent. The Jessie in question was a well-loved elephant at Sydney's Taronga Zoo.

the Hill 1. a sloping area of open ground for spectators at Flemington Racecourse, Melbourne. 2. a similar place that was formerly situated in front of the scoreboard at the Sydney Cricket Ground. 3. a local name for Broken Hill.

hissy fit an attack of hysterics; a temper tantrum.

home and hosed of a racehorse, having won by a great length. Hence, finished successfully, done with.

hoofa in WA, a slang name for Aussie Rules.

hooley dooley! an Australian exclamation of amazement or surprise. Also heard as **holy dooley**.

hoon 1. a hooligan or lout. The original sense, dating back to the 1930s. Origin unknown.

2. a fast, reckless driver of a car, boat, or the like. Now the most common meaning. Thus, a speedy drive, as in *I'm going out for a hoon tonight*. As a verb, to drive fast and recklessly.

hooray typically Aussie way of saying farewell. Recorded in the *Bulletin* way back in 1898. Also used in NZ. In origin this is merely an alteration of the word 'hurrah', which has also been used as a farewell. Unique to Australia is **hooroo**, and its unaspirated version, **ooroo**. This can be reliably dated back to 1916.

hop in for your chop to step up and take your fair share.

hops beer. Hence, **on the hops**, on a drinking binge.

hornbag someone who is sexually attractive and active.

horse's doover a jocular pronunciation of 'hors d'oeuvre'.

hottie 1. a hot-water bottle. **2.** a total hornbag.

how're you going? typical Aussie form of greeting. Does not require a precise answer. It's been in use since the 1930s at least. Another common form is **how's it going?** Or, more recently, **how're you travelling?** Elsewhere in the world they say 'How are you?'

Huey a jocular name for the powers above used when encouraging a heavy rainfall, or good snow or surf. *Send her down, Huey!* or *Whip 'em up, Huey!* Also spelt **Hughie**.

hump to carry. *He wandered up the hill humping a sack of potatoes.* To **hump the bluey** was to live the life of a swagman, carrying a swag and seeking work.

humpy any rough or temporary dwelling; a bush hut. Originally an Aboriginal dwelling. The word comes from the language Yagara of the Brisbane region.

hurl to vomit. Hence, an act of vomiting.

hydro 1. in Tas, short for the Hydro-Electric Commission. Hence, the power supplied them. The **hydro bill** is the electricity bill. **2.** hydroponically grown marijuana.

I

iceberg a regular winter swimmer; a strange individual who actually likes swimming in spanner water. An Australian institution since the 1930s.

-ie 1. a suffix used originally to create affectionate diminutives, as *doggie*, a dog; *littlie*, a child. This is common throughout all Englishes but in Australia we have really taken to it and use it to create slangy forms of ordinary words where the sense of smallness is not present, such as *Aussie*, an Australian; *brickie*, a bricklayer; *budgie*, a budgerigar; *conchie*, a conscientious objector; *goalie*, a goalkeeper; *mozzie*, a mosquito; and *truckie*, a truck driver. Often spelt **-y**, but in this dictionary the *-ie* form has been preferred for simplicity's sake. 2. used to form colloquial versions of place names, as *Charnie*, Charnwood, *Crowie*, Crows Nest, *Lonnie*, Launceston, *Winnie Hills*, Winston Hills. See the entry at **-o** for more information.

illywhacker a con artist or swindler. Dates back to underworld slang of the 1940s.

inked drunk, intoxicated.

in like Flynn assured of consummating a sexual encounter. Occasionally used in a non-sexual way to mean easily successful in a particular enterprise. Referring to Australian Hollywood actor Errol Flynn, notorious for his real-life sexual adventures. Interestingly this term has been used in the US since the 1940s, but only in the non-sexual sense.

in the chair being the person buying the drinks.

J

jack venereal disease. In origin from *jack in the box*, rhyming slang for 'pox'. Hence, to be **jacked-up**, is to be suffering from VD, which will require a visit to **the house that Jack built**, that is, the VD clinic.

jackaroo an apprentice station hand on a sheep or cattle station, especially one who wishes to learn how to manage a property. As a verb, to work as a jackaroo. *He's jackarooing in Queensland this year.* In use since the 1840s. The suggestion of an Aboriginal origin for this word is unfounded. Perhaps it is a blend of kangaroo with the male name Jack. A female of the species is, of course, a **jillaroo**.

Jack Lang Australian rhyming slang for 'Australian slang'. Jack Lang was a Labor premier of NSW twice in the 1920s and 1930s.

Jacky Howe a navy or black sleeveless woollen singlet traditionally worn by labourers and bushmen. Named after John Robert Howe, world champion shearer of 1892.

Jatz crackers the testicles. From rhyming slang for the 'knackers'.

Jeff in Victoria, to treat someone or something in the manner of Jeff Kennett, Liberal state premier from 1992 to 1999. Thus, to downsize, to reduce funding to, or to scrap an institution, government department, or the like; to retrench or fire staff; or generally, to ruin or destroy in a heartless and unfair way. *Our hopes of getting a fair wage deal have been Jeffed.*

Jeff's Shed in Vic, a derisive name for the Melbourne Exhibition Centre on the south bank of the Yarra.

jelly blubber a jellyfish.

jillaroo a female station hand on a sheep or cattle station. Modelled on **jackaroo**.

Jimmy dancer Aussie rhyming slang for 'cancer'. Dates back to the 1980s at least. Also, **disco dancer**, **Jack the dancer**, **Spanish dancer**, **tap dancer**.

Jimmy Woodser a person who drinks alone in a bar; also, a drink consumed alone. After 'Jimmy Wood' the loner in the 1892 poem of the same name by the bush balladist Barcroft Boake. Claims that it refers to an actual person have not been substantiated.

job to hit or punch. *I'll up and job the bastard.* A variant of the Standard English word *jab*. Hence, a punch or hit delivered. *He copped a hefty job on the nose.*

Joe Blake Aussie rhyming slang for 'snake'. Dates back to 1905. Also simply shortened to a **Joe**.

joey a disparaging term for an Anglo-Australian used by people of other ethnic background. Similar in origin, but not as common as, **skip** (see entry).

John Dory Aussie rhyming slang for 'story'. *What's the John Dory?* Dates back to the 1980s.

John Hop Aussie rhyming slang for 'cop', as in the police. Since the 1900s. Sometimes spelt **jonnop**.

joint 1. a place of business, especially a stall, tent, or small shop. 2. your house, unit, office, or the like. *Come round to my joint.* Can even be used to mean the entire country. *They come out here and act like they own the joint!*

joker a fellow or bloke. *He's a funny sort of joker.* An Australian original this one, recorded in the *Sydney Gazette* in 1810. Now used in the US.

jumbuck a sheep. Formerly quite common, now virtually obsolete except for its prominent placement in the national song *Waltzing Matilda*. Originally Aboriginal Pidgin English, where it seems as though it might be related to the phrase *jump up*. Apparently it was an Aboriginal belief that after dying they would 'Jump up, white fellow', that is, rise again reincarnated as a white person. Could it be that jumbuck is an alteration of *jump up*? Another theory has jumbuck as an Aboriginal word for 'a white mist preceding a shower', to which sheep supposedly bore a resemblance. A fanciful idea.

K

kangaroo **1.** To have **kangaroos loose in the top paddock** is to be slightly insane, a bit bonkers. Little known to most Aussies is that fact that across the Pacific Ocean in America they use the word kangaroo as well – as a derisive slang word for an Australian! **2.** to make a car jump along by unskilful clutch management. Also, **kangaroo-hop**. **3.** to squat over a toilet seat in order to do your business while avoiding contact with it.

Kangaroo Valley the suburb of Earls Court in London. It has long been the major haunt of yobbo tourists from Down Under.

kangawallafox a mythical monstrous beast, a cross between a kangaroo, a wallaby and a fox, tales of which are used to frighten tourists.

keep nit to act as a lookout, especially when an illegal activity is taking place. Also known as **keeping yow**.

keg-on-legs **1.** a person who drinks an inordinate amount of beer. **2.** an obese person.

keg party a traditional Aussie party at which a keg of beer is provided.

kelly a crow, a much hated bird in rural areas. Dating from the 1920s, this term is possibly wry reference to Ned Kelly, as a thief.

Kelly country a nickname for parts of north-eastern Vic and just across the border into NSW where the Kelly Gang operated.

Kenmore tractor Brisbane slang, a derogatory term for a city-only 4WD. See **Toorak tractor** for a host of synonyms.

kero typical laconic Aussie way of saying 'kerosene'.

Kickastickalong an imaginary remote country town.

kill a brown dog of food, to be disgustingly repulsive.

king brown in WA, a 750ml bottle of beer. Generally called a **long neck** elsewhere, except Qld, where the term **tallie** is favoured.

king hit originally, a knock-out blow. Now, a cowardly punch from behind. Hence, as a verb, to deliver such a blow. *He king-hit the boss and fled.* A **king hit merchant** is a cowardly thug whose MO is the king hit.

kip a sleep or nap. As a verb, to sleep. Hence, to stay somewhere on a temporary basis. *He's kipping at Tom's for a couple of days.*

knock-back a refusal or rejection. As a verb, **knock back**, to refuse.

knock 'em down rains violent thunderstorms in the Top End, with strong winds, lashing rain and plenty of lightning and thunder. Also called a **knock 'em down**. *Looks like we're in for another knock 'em down tonight.*

knocker 1. a person who's always putting others down; one who doesn't have anything good to say about anything. The kind of ratbag that Aussies have been hating under this title since at least the 1920s. 2. to be **on the knocker** is to be precisely accurate. *He was there at noon on the knocker.* It can also mean right away or immediately. *They want cash on the knocker.*

knuckle to assault with the fists. To **go the knuckle** is to fight. To be **fond of the knuckle** is to be keen on solving differences with the fists.

kylie 1. a boomerang having one flat and one convex side. From the Aboriginal language Nyungar of south-western WA. This is the origin of the popular Australian female name. 2. in south-western WA, a flat piece of metal shaped and thrown like a boomerang, used to catch fish in shallow waters.

L

Lady Blamey in World War II, a drinking glass made from an empty bottle with the top cut off. A string soaked in kerosene was wrapped around the bottle and then set alight. After the string had burnt through, the glass would separate where it was fire-weakened. This trick was taught to the troops by Lady Blamey, the wife of the commander of the south-western Pacific Allied Forces, Sir Thomas Blamey.

lady in the boat a cask of Coolabah moselle. It had a picture of a woman in a boat on the side.

lady's waist a small, waisted glass used for serving alcoholic drinks, formerly common in Australian pubs.

lagerphone a traditional Aussie folk music percussion instrument made from a stake to which beer bottle caps have been nailed. You bang it in time with the music.

lair a flashily dressed young man of brash and vulgar behaviour. Also known as a **mug lair**. Classic Aussie slang. This word is first recorded back in the 1920s and is a backformation from **lairy**.

lairise to behave like a lair; to show off; to indulge in exhibitionism. Original Aussie slang coined in the 1940s.

lambing down the practice of extracting the entire pay packet of a seasonal worker by getting them drunk and keeping them intoxicated until their money runs out. This reprehensible activity was commonplace in the outback in days of yore. The original meaning of **lamb down** is to tend ewes during lambing time.

land lice sheep.

Land of the Long Weekend Australia.

La Perouse Aussie rhyming slang for 'booze'. After the Sydney suburb south of Botany Bay. Named in honour of Comte de La Pérouse, the French navigator who narrowly missed claiming Australia for the French by showing up in Botany Bay about five days after Governor Phillip planted the Union Jack in Sydney Harbour.

lappies circuits of a street block in a car for the purpose of entertainment. This term is chiefly used in Qld. Compare **blockies** and **bog laps**.

Larry Dooley If you **give someone Larry Dooley**, it means you give them a hiding or beating.

lash an attempt. *I'll have a lash at it*.

laughing gear the mouth; to **wrap your laughing gear around** something is to eat it. *Here, wrap your laughing gear around this sanger*.

lazy wind a bitterly cold wind. It is too 'lazy' to go around you – it goes right through you instead.

leg opener an alcoholic drink calculated to facilitate the seduction of a woman.

lemon 1. a lesbian. Aussie slang from the 1980s, but perhaps earlier. So called because lemons are fruits (i.e. punning on *fruit* = homosexual). No doubt also influenced by the similarity of the first syllable of *le*mon and *le*sbian. **2.** a car which looks all right but actually is mechanically unsound. **3.** anything that is no good; a dud or turkey. **4.** a swindler's victim.

like a blue-arsed fly racing about furiously in a highly agitated state.

like a rat up a drainpipe with great speed. *I'd be up her like a rat up a drainpipe*. Also heard as **like a rat up a rope**.

lily on a dustbin a person or thing rejected or neglected. Hence, someone who looks incongruous, as being overdressed at an informal gathering.

lippie lipstick. Aussie women's slang since the 1950s. Also, **lippy**.

liquid laugh an act of vomiting, as you might experience after a lengthy liquid lunch.

liquid lunch alcoholic drink, usually beer, consumed instead of food at the normal lunchtime.

little Aussie battler a typical member of the working class in Australia.

the Little Digger nickname of Billy Hughes, the Australian Prime Minister during World War I.

Little Johnny a disparaging nickname for former Prime Minister John Howard. In reference to his small stature. He was also known as **Little Johnny Jackboots**.

lizard If you are working at full capacity or going at top speed, then you are **flat out like a lizard drinking**.

lob **1.** to arrive, especially unexpectedly. *He lobbed here this afternoon.* Also, **lob in** or **lob up**. **2.** to land. *My bag fell and lobbed on the rockery below.* **3.** to win a race. *He was hoping the horse would lob.*

lobster a twenty dollar note. So called from its colour.

local yokels the local inhabitants of a town, suburb, or the like.

logodile a half-submerged log mistaken for a crocodile.

lolly **1.** a sweet or piece of confectionery. A peculiarly Aussie (and NZ) term since the 1850s. **2.** money or dosh. *I'm running out of lolly.* **3.** the head. To **do your lolly** is to lose your temper.

lolly water carbonated soft drink. Sometimes used to refer to cordial.

London to a brick extremely likely. *It's London to a brick that he'll chicken out.* Coined by famous race caller Ken Howard who used it to unofficially announce winners in a tight finish while awaiting the official decision. In racing parlance it is a statement of betting odds in which a punter is so certain of the outcome that they are willing to bet London to win a measly brick (that is, ten quid). Technically the phrase should be 'London to a brick *on*'. Many people unaware of betting lingo leave out the vital word *on*, thus making the phrase the opposite of what is intended, i.e. the odds of laying a brick to win all of London. Not much of a risk.

long neck a 750ml bottle of beer. Also called a **longie**. In Qld they prefer the term **tallie**, and in WA, a **king brown**.

long streak of misery a tall, thin, miserable person.

lower than a snake's belly mean, despicable, contemptible.

lubricate the larynx to drink booze.

Lucky Country Australia seen as a fortunate country enjoying the benefits of prosperity, opportunity, stability, and the like. This appellation comes from the title of an influential book written in 1964 by Australian academic Donald Horne. It was originally intended by Horne as an ironic rebuke, describing Australians as having survived by 'luck' rather than good management – that we lazed around enjoying the good life, instead of concerning ourselves with productivity, international competitiveness, striving for the future, and stuff like that. Horne's negativeness was of course ignored by the average Aussie and the phrase has ended up being self-complimentary.

lunatic soup alcoholic drink; booze or grog.

lunch 1. to **cut someone's lunch** is to make a move on or steal their girlfriend or wife. Hence, a **lunch cutter** is someone who steals another's girlfriend. **2.** to **drop your lunch** or **open your lunch box** is to fart.

lurk a dodge; a slightly underhanded scheme. Commonly used in a positive way to refer to some easy way of making money. *He's on a good lurk.* Also frequently coupled with the word 'perk'. *She knows all the lurks and perks.*

M

maaate a long, drawn-out way of saying **mate**. Used in various contexts, such as a friendly greeting when two mates are pleased to see one another, as a way of cajoling a mate into agreeing with you, or as a way of placating a mate who is getting a bit hot under the collar.

mad as a cut snake extremely mad, either in the angry sense, or the crazy sense. Formerly it used to be just **mad as a snake**. Other great Aussie metaphors are **mad as a gumtree full of galahs** and **mad as a meat axe**.

Madonna's bra a local nickname for Sydney's Anzac Bridge – which, from a distance, vaguely resembles the pointy bra formerly worn by the pop star Madonna.

maggie an affectionate name for the magpie, a bird which during the breeding season will less than affectionately attack you.

maggoty in a bad mood.

Mainland in Tasmania this refers to continental Australia. However, if you are on King or Flinders Island then it refers to Tasmania. If you are from the Mainland, then you are, of course, a **Mainlander**.

mallee technically, a species of eucalyptus, but in slang **the mallee** refers to the remote outback, as in *Been stuck in the mallee for a week*. If you are as **fit as a mallee bull**, then you are superbly fit.

mango madness a feeling of oppression that descends upon residents of the Top End during the build-up to the wet season.

a man's not a camel! give me a drink before I die of thirst!

map of Tasmania the female pubic area. Also called the **map of Tassie**.

Marrickville Mercedes in Sydney, a derisive term for a Chrysler Valiant. Marrickville has a large ethnic population among whom this make of car is popular.

mate 1. a friend or cobber – the great Australian expression of true and undying friendship among men. Equivalent to the British *chum* and American *buddy* or *pal*. As in *They've been good mates from way back*, or *Never let a mate down*. This masculine bond is known as **mateship**, and almost made its way into our national Constitution. Anyhow, **mate** is a very serviceable word and is also commonly used as a form of address, as in *G'day mate* – and this can be said to someone who is a true mate, or just an acquaintance, or even someone you don't know but are meeting for the first time. **Mate** can also be used to refer to some bludger who isn't your mate in the slightest, as in *You got a problem with that, mate?* **2.** as applied to women by men, **mate** has for a long time, since at least the 1930s, been used to refer to a close female friend that a bloke does not have a romantic relationship with. Also, it is not too uncommon for men to refer to their wives as mates either: *Me missus is a great mate*. **3.** among women, at least in recent years, the traditional male usage has been adopted, so that a woman can refer to her female friends as *mates*.

Matilda a swag, hence the phrase **waltzing Matilda** means carrying your swag, in other words, being on the wallaby track, travelling from place to place looking for work. A lot of people blithely sing the song *Waltzing Matilda* without exactly knowing what the lyrics mean – which is a little bit funny since it is our national song after all.

metho **1.** methylated spirits. Also, **meths**. **2.** a metho drinker.

Mexican someone from 'south of the border'. So, in Qld, it can mean a person from New South Wales or Victoria, but in NSW, it means a person from Victoria.

Mickey Mouse **1.** rhyming slang for 'grouse' – excellent, terrific, wonderful. **2.** of a mechanical item, cheap and poorly made. Note how these two definitions are pretty much opposites – so you have to rely on context to get the meaning.

mint in WA, excellent, tops, terrific, cool. This was common from the 70s onwards. The idea is that mint is cool to the taste, and thus means 'cool', though it probably also owes something to the word 'mint' meaning in perfect condition. Anyhow, **mint** was later extended to become **mintox**, as in *That movie was mintox* or *I read a mintox book the other day*. This comes from the brand name of an oral antacid.

miserable as a ...

miserable as a bandicoot on a burnt ridge totally and utterly miserable.

missus 1. the wife; the little woman; the cheese and kisses. 2. the woman of the house on a rural property or station, traditionally having jurisdiction over the affairs pertaining to the homestead. Counterpart to the **boss**.

mob 1. a group of people, as friends, not necessarily large. *We'll invite the mob over for Saturday night.* 2. in Aboriginal English, a tribal or language group, or a community. 3. If there are **mobs of** something or some things, then there is a lot of it, or a large number of them. If there are still more, then it is a **big mob**, and an even larger number is denoted by **biggest mob**. *There were big mobs of people at the race meeting. I'll have big mobs of mashed potato, please. Biggest mob of cattle over that hill!*

mocker to **put the mocker on** is to jinx or bring bad luck to someone. You can also **put the mockers on** or **put the mocks on** someone.

mollydooker a left-handed person. Probably from British dialect *molly* 'an effeminate man' and *dook* 'the hand'.

mongrel 1. a detestable person. 2. something difficult. *It's a mongrel of a job.* 3. despicable; detestable; rotten; ratshit. *You filthy rotten mongrel bastard.*

moonbeam a plate, cup or piece of cutlery which was not used at an evening meal, and does not need washing up. The night-time equivalent of the **sunbeam**.

more front than Myers overly impudent. From the Melbourne department store which has a large frontage. A similar phrase is **more hide than Jessie**, referring to a well-known elephant formerly at Sydney's Taronga zoo.

Mosman tractor Sydney slang, a derogatory term for a city-only 4WD that never sees off-road driving. Also known as a **Mosman shopping trolley** or a **Mosman truck**. See **Toorak tractor** for a host of synonyms.

mouth like the bottom of a cocky's cage the sort of mouth you get after a big night out on the grog.

move it, or lose it a warning indicating that one should move whatever it is one has in the way.

mow someone's lawn to have sex with another's partner; to cuckold someone. Also, to **cut someone's grass**.

mozzie a mosquito. Aussie slang from the 1930s. Also spelt **mossie**.

mud gecko a crocodile.

mud map a map drawn in the earth with a stick. Common out in the bush.

muffin top a bulbous protrusion of bouncy blubber to be found squeezed out of the top of too-tight hipster jeans.

mug 1. a fool. Hence, stupid, as in the *mug punters* or a *mug copper*. 2. a criminal's victim or 'mark'; also, anyone who is not a member of the underworld. 3. the face.

mug's game a foolish enterprise; an occupation a mug is likely to get involved in. *Gambling is a mug's game*, *Married life is a mug's game*.

mulga technically, any of several species of acacia, but in slang **the mulga** means the outback. *She's been out in the mulga for a few years*.

mulga wire the rural gossip mill; the bush telegraph.

mungo a derogatory term for a Rugby League player. Been around since the 1960s. It is also used to mean a player who has committed the sin of switching from Union to League. Sometimes it's pronounced **mongo**. The origin of the term remains a mystery though many have sought it. The mostly likely is that it is derived from *mongrel*.

Murrumbidgee whaler a swagman who frequented the Australian inland rivers and sustained himself by both begging and fishing. A *whaler* was a person who fished for Murray cod.

muso a musician.

my dog's are barking my feet are sore. From British rhyming slang *dog's meat* = feet.

mystery bag 1. a sausage. 2. a meat pie. Also called a **mystery box**. Not to be confused with the **mystery bundle**, that is, a pastie.

my word You bet! Certainly! An original Australianism dating as far back as the 1850s.

N

nana a banana. To **chuck a nana** is to throw a tantrum. This is also known as **doing your nana**. If you are **off your nana** you are crazy.

nark 1. a police informer. 2. a whingeing, whining person; one who is always interfering and spoiling the pleasure of others; a spoilsport or wowser. 3. to irritate or annoy. *Jack'll be narked about this*. Hence, to be **narky** is to be irritable or bad-tempered.

national game Actually, Australia has two national games – **Aussie Rules** and **two-up**.

naughty an act of sexual intercourse. A ridgy-didge Australianism first recorded in 1959.

neddy a horse. Aussie slang since the 1880s. In early British slang this was used for a donkey – Australians seem to have borrowed the word but changed the meaning. Hence, the **neddies** are the horseraces.

Ned Kelly Australia's most famous bushranger and unofficial national hero. Used in a negative way to refer to anyone who is a bit of a crook, or in a positive way to mean a person who courageously stands up against overbearing authority. To be **game as Ned Kelly** is to be outstandingly gutsy. If you are **in more shit than Ned Kelly**, then you are in big strife.

never-never sparsely inhabited outback regions of Australia. Aussie slang since the 1830s.

Neville an unpopular person; a nerd, dag or geek. Same as a **Nigel**.

new chum 1. originally, a newly transported convict; later, any newly arrived immigrant from Britain. The butt of much humour and scorn because of their naivety regarding Australian life and ways. This term was first used at the beginning of the 19th century, but began to die out in this sense in the first decades of the 20th. The opposite was, naturally, the **old chum**. 2. a novice or inexperienced person. *I was the new chum on the job*. This meaning first appears in the 1850s and is still in use.

nick **1.** prison. In British slang it is used for the police station. **2.** to capture or arrest. **3.** to steal. **4.** to go or move with speed. *I'll nick across the road.*

nick out to go out for a short period. *I'll just nick out and get a few things from the shops.*

Nigel an unpopular person; a nerd, dag or geek. Same as a **Neville**. Also known as **Nigel No-Friends**.

nipper **1.** a small child; a kid. **2.** a young lad on a construction site or in a mine who does small odd jobs, such as making tea and buying lunch. **3.** a junior lifesaver.

nit a word used to warn people engaged in some illegal activity that the police are coming. Thus, to **keep nit** is to keep watch or act as a lookout. Recorded in Australia from as early as 1882.

nit keeper a person who keeps watch for authorities while illegal activities are taking place; a lookout or cockatoo.

Noah's ark **1.** rhyming slang for 'shark'. Aussie slang since the 1940s. Commonly shortened to **Noah**. **2.** rhyming slang for 'nark', as in a spoilsport. Much older this one, dating back to the 1890s, but now obsolete.

no Arthur Murrays Aussie rhyming slang for 'no worries'. From the famous Arthur Murray Dance Studios.

no David Murrays South Australian rhyming slang for 'no worries'. From David Murray's, a well-known furniture store in Adelaide.

no flies on you a complimentary phrase meaning you are clever. This is one Australianism that has made its way to the US.

no good to gundy no good at all. Who (or what) 'Gundy' was has been lost in time.

no-hoper **1.** an unpromising racehorse or greyhound; an outsider. **2.** a hopeless case. *He is a real no-hoper at tennis.* Borrowed into the US in the 1950s.

nointer in Tasmania, a mischievous child or brat. From British dialect, a shortening of *anointer* 'a mischievous fellow'. This relates to 19th century dialect verb *anoint* 'to chastise or thrash', in other words to 'consecrate' by beating – they had funny religious ideas back in those days.

nong a fool or idiot; a drongo. A shortening of **ning-nong**.

no risk! an exclamation of reassurance or approval. Aussie slang dating from the late

1950s – slightly earlier than **no worries**.

norks breasts. First recorded in the 1960s. Also rarely found in the form **norgs**. The suggestion that it is from *Norco* butter, the wrapping of which at one time featured a cow's udder, is barely worth consideration. Origin unknown.

the North Island in Tasmania, an ironic nickname for the Mainland.

North Shore tank Sydney slang, a derogatory term for a city-only 4WD. Also called a **North Shore Kingswood**. See **Toorak tractor** for a host of synonyms.

nosebag to **put on the nosebag** is to begin a meal.

not happy Jan! a phrase expressing irritation, annoyance or disapproval. From the 2002 Yellow Pages advertising campaign in which a manager realises that her staff member 'Jan' has neglected to place an ad in time.

not have a bar of to have nothing to do with; to totally repudiate.

not know from a bar of soap to be completely unfamiliar with. *He doesn't know me from a bar of soap.*

not much chop no good. Aussie slang since the 1840s. From *first chop* 'highest quality', a term originating in the Anglo-Indian English of the Raj, and ultimately coming from Hindi *chāp* 'a stamp or brand'.

not the sharpest tool in the shed not very bright.

no worries **1.** don't you worry about that! *No worries, trust me, I'm good!* **2.** don't mention it! you're welcome! *'Thanks for bringing those beers over.' 'No worries, mate.'*

number ones urination.

number twos defecation.

nut case a foolish or eccentric person.

nut out to work out or solve. World War I Aussie slang.

O

-o 1. a suffix used to create slangy forms of ordinary words and names. First used in occupational names of itinerant street vendors such as the *rabbit-o* and *bottle-o*. Such vendors announced their arrival by crying out their wares followed by 'oh' – *Rabbit Oh!*, *Bottle Oh!*, *Milk Oh!*, etc. Later it was added to the first syllable of multisyllabic words, such as *arvo*, afternoon; *compo*, compensation; *demo*, demonstration; *kero*, kerosene; *muso*, musician; *panno*, panel wagon; *reffo*, refugee; *Salvo*, Salvation Army officer; and *smoko*, smoking break. The **-o** suffix alternates with the **-ie** suffix, which is used in pretty much the same manner, though often with a diminutive sense as well. Very few words can take both suffixes – *alko/alkie, arvo/arvie, flanno/flannie, lammo/lammie* and *sammo/sammie* are a few of the exceptions. Of course, there is a very big difference between a *sicko* and a *sickie*! Knowing just when to use the **-o** and when the **-ie** suffix is a skill that defines whether or not someone is a natural speaker of Australian English. **2.** used in positive responses or assurances, as *good-o* and *righto*. **3.** used to form colloquial versions of personal names, especially male names, as *Gibbo*, Gibson, *Tommo*, Thompson, *Davo*, Dave, *Peto*, Peter. **4.** used to form colloquial versions of place names, as *Baulko*, Baulkham Hills, *Belco*, Belconnen, *Ermo*, Ermington, *Penno*, Pennant Hills.

ocker 1. the archetypal uncultivated Australian working man. Also spelt with a capital, **Ocker**. Generally used in a negative way to depict a chauvinistic, misogynistic, sports-loving, beer-gutted, esky-carrying, rubber-thong-wearing yob. Totally lacking in sensitivity, compassion, gentleness and insight. Exactly the same 'bloke' can be seen also in a positive way, as an honest, laid-back, fair dinkum, fun-loving larrikin. An Australian cult figure – popularly satirised in the 1970s by the likes of Paul Hogan and the Barry Humphries creation Bazza McKenzie. In origin, the term derives from the typically Aussie way of colloquialising the name Oscar. From as early as 1916 blokes named Oscar were called Ocker. In the late 1960s a TV comedy called *The Mavis Bramston Show* had a character named Ocker, played by Barry Creyton, who was your typical uncultivated Australian male, and it is probably from this show that the word was first disseminated throughout the country. As an adjective, **ocker** has come to mean quintessentially Australian. *He had an ocker sense of humour.* And although principally designating men, it can also be used of women. *She was ocker through and through.* **2.** Australian English. *I lapsed into ocker and yelled 'Dice it!'*

ockerdom the society of boorish, uncouth, chauvinistic Australians.

ockie strap an octopus strap.

off like a bride's nightie off or away with the utmost speed.

off like a bucket of prawns in the midday sun extremely rotten; stinking.

oil news or information. As 'oil' lubricates a machine, so 'information' greases the wheels of progress. Generally qualified in some way, as **dinkum oil**, **good oil**, **inside oil** and **straight oil**.

oil the tonsils to drink booze. Also heard in the form **oil the larynx**.

old chum in colonial times, an experienced colonist, a person who had spent some years in the colony, especially in the outback, and was thus accustomed to Australian life and conditions. The opposite of **new chum** (see entry).

the Old Dart England. Has been used in Australia since the 1890s. Dart is the same word as 'dirt', as pronounced in the Essex dialect of southern England. Thus Old Dart = Old Dirt, a person's native land.

olds your parents. Aussie slang from the 1970s.

on a good wicket in a great position; successful or poised for success.

the One Day of the Year Anzac Day, the 25th April.

one for Ron a cigarette borrowed for later on. (Get it? – Later Ron). *Can I have a ciggie, and one for Ron?*

one-pub town a small country town with only one pub. A term first used by Henry Lawson. If it's slightly bigger it might be termed a **two-pub town**, in which case you will invariably have a **top pub** and a **bottom pub**, nomenclature that is only immediately clear to the locals!

on for young and old wild, unrestrained and involving everyone – used of a fight, argument, or the like.

on the bugle stinking to high heaven. The bugle here is, of course, the nose.

on the land working as a farmer.

on the Murray cod Aussie rhyming slang for 'on the nod', that is, on credit – used of wagers.

on the nose 1. smelly, stinking. *Man, this bait's a bit on the nose!* 2. unpleasant, distasteful.

onya an abbreviated form of *good on you!* Also, in the plural, **onyas**. Been around since the 1940s.

on your hammer following closely, or, when in a vehicle, tailgating. From *hammer and tack*, rhyming slang for 'back'.

on your Pat Malone Aussie rhyming slang for 'on your own'. Commonly shortened to **on your Pat**. Dates back to the 1900s.

Oodnawoopwoop an imaginary remote town. *His parents had a station out Oodnawoopwoop.* A blend of *Woop Woop* and *Oodnadatta*, which is a fairly remote town in north central SA, far from Adelaide. Another similar remote and backward town is **Oodnagalahbi**.

oo-roo Goodbye! See ya! An unaspirated version of the more common **hooroo**.

optic nerve Aussie rhyming slang for 'perv'. Commonly shortened to **optic**. *Give us an optic at that.*

oscar ready money. Short for *Oscar Asche*, rhyming slang for 'cash'. Aussie slang dating from the 1900s. Oscar Asche was a famous actor and stage producer who died in 1936.

othersider in WA, a person living on the other side of the Nullarbor Plain.

outback the remote, sparsely inhabited parts of Australia. The symbolic heart of the nation. The term first appears in the 1890s. An inhabitant of this region is occasionally called an **outbacker**. And bush life and ways are sometimes termed **outbackery**.

outlaws a joking term for your in-laws.

Oz Australia or Australian. Has been around since the 1940s, but only became common from the 1970s onwards.

P

pack of poo tickets **1.** something that is in an unholy mess. For an explanation of this term see **pakapoo ticket**. **2.** a roll of toilet paper. This meaning seems to have arisen through a complete ignorance of the original term.

paddock **1.** a sporting field. **2.** a spectator's enclosure at a racetrack.

paddock-basher **1.** an old car, generally unregistered, used for driving around paddocks. **2.** any old bomb for bashing around the bush. Such rough-and-ready driving is called **paddock-bashing**. For short, such cars can be called **paddy-bashers**.

paddy wagon a police van for transporting people under arrest.

pakapoo ticket Something that is in an unholy mess, especially written work, is said to look like a **pakapoo ticket**. Aussie slang since the 1950s. This originally referred to the tickets used in a type of Chinese gambling game, which were marked with Chinese characters. To western eyes, they just looked like messy scribble. The game was recorded in Australia from as early as 1886. Through mishearing the term, some people have come to say **pack of poo tickets** (see entry).

panic merchant an inveterate panicker; a worry wart.

papers cigarette papers. Nowadays most commonly called **tally-hos**, after a popular brand. In Tasmania called **tissues**.

paralytic completely drunk.

park the carcass to take a seat.

pash **1.** a long, passionate, deep kiss. Aussie slang from the 1960s onwards. **2.** a session of passionate kissing, especially French kissing. **3.** to kiss passionately; to French kiss; to suck face. Hence, **pash on**, to have a prolonged kissing session, and **pash off**, to kiss someone until fully satisfied.

pash rash raw red skin around the mouth caused by overly amorous pashing, especially with an unshaven man. Also, **gravel rash**.

passion wagon a panel van used as a place of sexual encounter.

pav laconic Australian way of saying 'pavlova'.

pearler something exceptional or superlative. *Her new dress was a real pearler.* In cricket, a very good delivery. Sometimes spelt **purler**.

peg 1. to throw or toss something. Most common in Qld and NSW. An Aussie original. Recorded since the 1940s. 2. to observe, look or watch. Hence, to comprehend the true nature of someone. *I've got you pegged.* 3. a look or peek. *Have a peg at this.*

perv 1. a sexual pervert; a person with an abnormal kink. Obviously a shortening of the word *pervert*. Also spelt **perve**. Hence, a leering, voyeuristic man; anyone whose sexual advances are unwanted. *Rack off, you old perv.* 2. an act of voyeurism; a look taken for the sake of sexual observation. *Just having a bit of a perv.* 3. an attractive person; one who is worth perving at. 4. to watch a person lustfully; to look at someone in a sexual way. 5. to look or gawk at (but not in a sexual way). *They all just stood around perving at the couple fighting.*

petrol head a car nut.

piano arms the arms of an overweight or matronly woman with flabby triceps.

piece to **take a piece out of** someone is to chastise or rebuke them.

pie-eater a person of little or no importance. Metaphorically referring to a person whose narrow view of the world is given away by the fact that they eat nothing but meat pies. Has been around since the 1940s.

pike 1. to **pike on** someone is to let them down or abandon them. *Don't pike on me now.* 2. to **pike out** is to go back on an arrangement or to opt out of something in a cowardly manner. *He piked out on the deal.*

piker 1. a person who in a cowardly fashion opts out of an arrangement or challenge; a person who lets you down at the last moment. In Australia, pikers are pretty low down on the scale of things. 2. a timid gambler who hasn't the guts to risk big money.

pill in Aussie Rules and Rugby, the football.

ping **1.** to penalise for an infringement of the rules. *I got pinged for holding my player.* **2.** of a racehorse, to put on a sudden burst of speed. *About 200 metres out she pinged for the line.*

pinnies pinball machines.

piss **1.** to urinate. Also, as a noun, urine or urination. Actually, although very old, this is technically not one of the original Anglo-Saxon four-letter words, as it originally came into medieval English from Old French. If you have a low regard for someone you **wouldn't piss on them**. If you have even less regard you **wouldn't piss on them if they were on fire**. Utter contempt can further be expressed by saying you **wouldn't piss in their ear if their brain was on fire**. **2.** as a noun, urine or an act of urination. *I'm hanging for a piss.* An insignificant amount of something is styled **a piss in the ocean**, and something easily achieved is **a piece of piss** or **a piece of piss to a trained digger**. **3.** alcoholic drink, especially beer. Hence, **on the piss**, on a binge. **4.** to **take the piss out of** someone is to stir or make fun of them. **5.** used as an intensifier, the word **piss** can be prefixed to the beginning of adjective. *That was piss-awful* = extremely awful. Also, can be substituted for 'the hell', as in *He scared the piss out of me.*

pissed drunk. There are numerous similes, the most common in Australia probably being **pissed as a parrot** (not that parrots are known for their drinking habits) – this has been around since the 1970s and seems to be an Aussie original. But you can be **pissed as a bastard/fart/newt/owl**, or **pissed as forty arseholes**. You can also be **pissed to the eyeballs**.

piss in someone's pocket to flatter someone; to ingratiate yourself to someone. Aussie slang since the 1940s.

piss it in to win easily.

Pitt Street farmer in NSW, a person who owns a country property, often for purposes of tax avoidance, but who lives and works in Sydney. See **Collins Street cocky**, **Queen Street bushie**.

plonk cheap wine. Can be used jokingly to refer to really excellent wine. *That's not a bad bottle of plonk you've got there.* Originally Aussie slang, first recorded in the 1930s. Probably a corrupt pronunciation of French *blanc*, as in *vin blanc* 'white wine'. Possibly originating with Australian troops in France in World War I.

Now commonly used in Britain.

plonko an alcoholic who drinks wine. Also called a **plonkie**.

plumber's smile the portion of a buttock cleft showing above the top of someone's pants; the coin slot. Also called the **plumber's crack** or the **plumber's bike rack**.

poddy-dodge to steal unbranded cattle. Hence a proponent of this is known as a **poddy-dodger**.

poisoner a cook, especially a shearers' cook.

pokies poker machines.

pollie a politician.

pollywaffle a floating piece of human excrement in the water you are swimming in. From the brand name of a chocolate bar. See **blind mullet** for a swag of synonyms.

Pom usual abbreviation of **Pommy**.

Pommy a term, sometimes derogatory, for an English

plumber's smile

Pommy

person. It first appears in documentary evidence in 1912 and was originally used to refer to immigrants from Britain (not only England), as opposed to long-term or native-born Australian residents. For a long time Pommy was quite derogatory, but nowadays it carries less negative connotations than it used to and can even be used affectionately. As for the origin – well, the much repeated suggestion that it derives from an acronym of Prisoner Of Mother England (POME), or Prisoner Of Her Majesty (POHM), or any other of numerous variants is clearly wrong – it is nothing but urban legend. Firstly, there is no documentary evidence of such phrases and acronyms ever being in use. Secondly, acronyms were extremely rare before the 1950s. Thirdly, the period of transportation had been over for about 75 years before the word Pommy ever appeared. Fourthly, the word Pommy was applied to immigrants and never to convicts or prisoners. The actual source of the word is *pomegranate*, rhyming slang for 'immigrant'. This piece of home-grown rhyming slang first appears in 1912, the same time that both *Pommy* and *Pom* arrive on the scene, hence the conclusion that the latter two are abbreviations of the first is unavoidable.

pork chop **1.** to be **silly as a pork chop** is to be really, really silly. Similarly, to **carry on like a pork chop** is to behave in a silly fashion. Why pork chops are especially silly, as opposed to other cuts of meat, is one of those unanswerable mysteries of slang. **2.** something unwanted is said to be **like a pork chop at a Jewish wedding.**

possie a place or position. *Save me a possie next to you.* Also spelt **pozzie**. Originally World War I digger slang which referred to a position or shelter, or a hiding place taken up by a sniper.

possum **1.** to **stir the possum** is to create a disturbance. **2.** a term of affectionate address. *How are you, possum?* Popularised by Dame Edna Everage.

possum stomp to jump up and down on with large boots.

potato **1.** a woman or girl. From *potato peeler*, rhyming slang for 'sheila'. **2.** a small hole in a sock through which skin is showing.

pov **1.** poor. A shortening of the word 'poverty'. Hence, a poor person. *They're such povs they can't afford new thongs.* Recent Aussie slang from the 1990s.

2. bad, pathetic, uncool. Used chiefly by adolescents who associate poverty with lack of sophistication, style, and the like – kids can be so cruel. Also, **povvo** or **povvy**.

pox doctor a doctor treating venereal disease. If you are **all dressed up like a pox doctor's clerk**, then you are dressed in a flashy manner that reveals a rather poor taste in clothing.

prawn **1.** a fool or jerk; an insignificant or objectionable person. *He's a bit of a prawn.* Australian slang since the 1890s. Also called a **prawn head**. See also the phrase **don't come the raw prawn**. **2.** a person with an nice body but an ugly head. **3.** to be **off like a bucket of prawns** is to be really rotten; to stink.

pull on the wobbly boots to prepare yourself for going out and getting drunk.

pull your head in! Mind your own business!

pure merino a member of an old and established Australian family not of convict descent.

push **1.** formerly, a gang of vicious city hooligans. Known by the area they frequented, as 'the Rocks push' or the 'Cardigan Street push'. Especially common in the 19th century and early 20th century. **2.** a group of friends or associates.

put some wood in the hole please shut the door!

put the acid on to pressure someone into doing something they are reluctant to do, especially to come across with sexual favours.

put the hard word on to be persistent in asking for a favour. Aussie slang since World War I. Often used specifically to refer to sexual favours. *The boss put the hard word on the new secretary.* This nuance has been around since at least the 1930s.

Q

quack originally a swindler who claimed to be a medical practitioner and sold cure-alls or other fabulous medicines, but in Australia any doctor at all – with the joking implication that they are all phoneys. First used during World War I.

Queen Street bushie in Qld, one who owns a country property, often for purposes of tax avoidance, but who lives and works in Brisbane. Can be used to mean any wannabe farmer. Also called a **Queen Street ringer**. See **Pitt Street farmer**, **Collins Street cocky**.

quickie 1. sex on the fly, and often through the fly. 2. a quick drink. 3. anything done rapidly or in a short space of time.

quid 1. Despite its demise as a term for currency, quid still lingers in a number of slang expressions. For example, someone who is lacking in intelligence is said to be **not the full quid**. 2. money, especially a large amount. *It must have cost a quid*. A **quick quid** is a modest amount of money earned with little effort. If you won't do something **for quids**, then you won't do it under any circumstances. *I wouldn't miss it for quids*. And, finally, the great Aussie expression of lust for life: **I wouldn't be dead for quids**.

quince To **get on someone's quince** is to annoy or irritate them.

quokka soccer the so-called 'sport' of kicking quokkas on Rottnest Island. The small endangered marsupial known as the quokka still exists in large numbers only on fox-free Rottnest Island about 12km off the coast from Perth. Each year post-exam schoolkids descend on the island and get roaring drunk – and thus quokka soccer was invented. The local population of quokkas were used to people as some 400,000 tourists a year visit the island – and so they were fair game for drunken youths. They usually die from internal injuries after being kicked. The sadistic practice is now banned and warrants a $10,000 fine.

R

rabbit 1. a fool. 2. in cricket, a player who is not very good at batting. Also called a **bunny**. Neither of which are as bad as being the **ferret** (see entry).

racehorse 1. a thinly rolled cigarette or joint. So called because it is smoked quickly. Originally prison slang. 2. in WA, a sand goanna.

race off To **race someone off** is to take them to a secluded spot for sex. *He races his wife off to the bedroom as much as possible.*

Rafferty's rules no rules at all. Probably a use of the Irish surname as a slur on their supposed unruliness.

rainbow dozen a mixed dozen of the range of Cascade beers (Blue, Red, Green).

rainmaker in Aussie Rules, a very high kick.

rashie a lycra garment worn under a wetsuit for prevention of rash; a rash vest.

ratbag 1. a worthless, despicable, unreliable person. Aussie slang. Recorded as early as 1890, but not common until the 1940s. 2. an eccentric or queer person; a weirdo. Hence, **ratbaggery**.

rat house a psychiatric hospital.

rat on stilts a racing greyhound.

rat's coffin a meat pie.

rats with wings a derogatory term for the much hated feral pigeons that infest Australian cities and towns.

rattler any of various types of trains noted for their loud rattling. To **jump a rattler** was to board a moving train and thus obtain a ride without buying a ticket – a practice common among swagmen during the Depression.

rattle your dags Hurry up! Get a move on! A **dag** is a lump of excrement-matted wool on a sheep's rear – this command evokes an image of a dag-laden sheep being given a hurry-up.

razoo a fictional coin of little value. To have no money is to **not have a razoo**, and to be worth nothing is to be **not worth a razoo**. Commonly called a **brass razoo**. Such a coin never existed. The origin of this term has led to much speculation over the years, most of which is not worth a brass razoo. However, one intriguing possibility is that it is a euphemistic alteration of *arse razoo* = a fart. The word *razoo* was used in American slang since the late 19th century to mean a fart, being a variant of *raspberry*, from rhyming slang, *raspberry tart* 'fart'.

Razzle an RSL club. Also **the Razza**.

red-back a twenty dollar note.

red can a can of Melbourne Bitter beer. As opposed to a **blue**, **green**, **white** or **yellow can** (see entries).

red handbag a cask of cheap red wine. Also called a **red suitcase**.

red ned cheap red wine.

red rattler any of various passenger trains with dark red carriages which rattled noisily when travelling at speed.

Reg Grundies Aussie rhyming slang for 'undies'. After *Reg Grundy*, Oz television producer. Also called **Reggies**, **Reginalds** or **Grundies**.

rat's coffin

rellie a relative. Also common in the form **rello**. One of the few words which have both an *-ie* and an *-o* form. Your relatives are also known as the **rels**.

rev head a car enthusiast.

ridgy-didge 1. true, genuine, dinkum. First recorded in the 1950s. This great ockerism comes from the earlier *ridge* = genuine, which dates back to the 1930s, and probably comes from underworld slang *ridge* = gold or gold coins. 2. Aussie rhyming slang for 'fridge'. *Just whack it in the ridgy-didge.*

ringer 1. the fastest shearer in a shearing shed. Recorded since the 1870s. This word comes from an earlier, now obsolete, sense, where a ringer was any person or thing that was superlatively good. For more information see the entry for **snagger**. 2. a stockman or drover. So called because they circle the stock and keep them together. Dates back to the 1900s. 3. a substitute racehorse or greyhound; a ring-in or ringtail. Aussie racing slang since the 1930s.

ring-in 1. a racehorse or greyhound substituted for another in a race. 2. a person or thing substituted for another at the last moment. *Joe couldn't come, so I'm the ring-in.* 3. a person pretending to be someone else; a phoney. 4. someone from another place; an outsider.

ripper something or someone exciting extreme admiration. *You little ripper!* Also used as an adjective to mean absolutely excellent. *It's a ripper movie.* Originally 19th century British slang, but has since died out there. It has been used in Australia since the 1850s.

rissole 1. an RSL club. Chiefly NSW slang. Hence, for entertainers to **do the rissoles** is to make a tour of RSL clubs. 2. If someone farewells you with 'See ya round', the stock reply is 'Yeah, like a rissole.'

roadie 1. a bottle or can of beer consumed while driving. Also called a **traveller**. 2. a measure of driving distance equivalent to the distance travelled while consuming one bottle or can of beer. *It's a three-roadie trip.* 3. one for the road. *Have you got time for a roadie?*

rock hopper a person who fishes from coastal rocks.

rock lobster a twenty dollar note. So called from its colour.

roll 1. to convince a person to turn witness and incriminate others. 2. a bankroll. This dates back to the mid-19th century. In Australia a very big bankroll can be described as

a roll so big Jack Rice couldn't jump over it. Jack Rice was the name of a successful steeplechase and hurdles racehorse of the 1910s.

rollie a hand-rolled cigarette; a roll-your-own.

roo 1. a kangaroo. This shortening dates back to the 1890s. Commonly spelt with an apostrophe, **'roo**. 2. a jackaroo. This shortening also dates back to the 1890s.

roo bar a bullbar fitted to the front of a vehicle. Necessary in the outback to deflect roos without causing too much damage to said vehicle – well, that's the idea.

a rooster one day and a feather duster the next a phrase expressive of the ups and downs of life.

ropeable seething with anger; literally, 'fit to be tied'. Aussie slang from the 1870s, and still going strong.

rort a trick, lurk, or underhand scheme; a confidence trick. Hence, as a verb, to swindle, dupe or gyp. In origin a back-formation from **rorty** meaning 'wild and rowdy', as a party or the like. In fact, back in the 1950s and 60s a **rort** was a wild party, but this meaning has died out. In this day and age **rort** is commonly used of election rigging, embezzlement, and other dodgy practices indulged in by the nation's shakers and movers – and in this sense the word is hardly slang any more. It can also be used to describe a job that's a bit of a bludge. *Nice rort you're on here*.

rorter a person who perpetrates a rort; a con artist or swindler.

Rose Bay shopping trolley Sydney slang, a derogatory term for a city-only 4WD that never sees off-road driving. See **Toorak tractor** for a host of synonyms.

rotten extremely drunk.

rough as bags extremely rough, uncouth, dirty, and ugly to boot. Variations include **rough as guts** and **rough as hessian undies** – Ouch!

rough end of the pineapple a raw deal; the worst part of a bargain.

rough trot a spell of bad luck or misfortune.

rouse on to scold or upbraid. You can also **rouse at** someone. In origin, a variant of Scottish *roust* 'shout or roar'.

rubbish to denigrate or put down.

rubbity-dub Aussie rhyming slang for 'pub'. Been around since the 1890s. Commonly shortened to **rubbity**. Also, **rub-a-dub-dub**.

rugger bugger a derogatory term for a Rugby Union player seen as the bastion of coarse tastes and loud behaviour.

rum 'un in Tasmania, an eccentric person, a character or wag, a cheeky person or scallywag. Formerly common all over the country but now restricted principally to Tasmania. Also spelt **rumun** and **rumin**. From *rum* 'odd' and *'un* 'one'. Aussie slang from the 1890s, but ultimately from British dialect.

rust bucket a badly rusted motor vehicle.

S

salmon a twenty dollar note. From its orange colour.

saltie a saltwater crocodile.

Salvo a member of the Salvation Army. Aussie slang since the 1890s. Hence, **the Salvos**, the Salvation Army. The synonymous **Sallie** arrived on the scene much, much later.

sambo a sandwich. Also **sammo** or, with the *-ie* ending, either **sambie** or **sammie**.

sandgroper a derisive term for a Western Australian. This has been around since the 1890s. See **cornstalk** for similar terms of derision for people from other states.

sanger **1.** a sandwich. From the pronunciation 'sangwich'. **2.** a sausage. Also spelt **sanga**.

schmick **1.** cool, excellent, terrific; classy and stylish. *He's got a really schmick car*. Also spelt **smick**, or extended with the Aussie *-o* ending to **schmicko**. **2.** neat, tidy, in good nick. In the armed forces, commonly used to refer to immaculate attire or drill. Perhaps from German *schmuck* 'neat', 'spruce', 'smart'. **3.** as a verb, to do up beautifully; to get spruced up. *We got all schmicked up for the photos*.

schoolie a school student. Specifically, a holidaying school student who has just completed their final year exams; a teenager on a holiday during schoolies week.

schoolies week a week or so of holiday, taken by Year 12 students after their final exams.

scone the head. Hence, as a verb, to strike on the head. *Sconed him a beauty with a wet tennis ball*.

Scott Neville an unpopular bloke; a real loser; a complete dag. *Check out the Scott Neville sitting under the tree by himself*. So called because 'He's got no mates, and never will'.

scozzer a Victorian term for a bogan, bevan or westie. Also spelt **scozza**, or even better, **skozza**. Origin unknown.

screamer a remarkable or superlative thing. In surfing, a large wave. In Aussie Rules, a spectacular mark. *He pulled down a terrific screamer, right on the buzzer.*

scrub bashing driving a vehicle through virgin bush. Also called **bush bashing**.

scrub up to appear as specified, after grooming. *She scrubs up pretty well.*

scum to cadge something. *He was trying to scum a cigarette.*

scungy mean, dirty, miserable, unpleasant. Australian and NZ slang since the 1960s. Also sometimes spelt **skungy**.

servo a service station.

session 1. a booze-up. 2. the hours on Sunday during which a particular pub is open – the **Sunday session**. Especially common in WA. Can also refer to Saturday if the pub has restricted hours on that day. 3. a dope smoking session. 4. a period of surfing, normally a couple of hours.

shag on a rock a lonely person. *All alone like a shag on a rock.* Referring to the shag or cormorant, a black marine bird commonly seen perched alone on seaside rocks. An Australian simile dating back to the 1840s.

shanghai 1. a child's catapult. Recorded in Australia since the 1860s. Perhaps this word comes from the Scottish word *shangie* 'a cleft stick put onto a dog's tail' – however, that word was pronounced 'shan-gee', which is quite a way from 'shang-eye'. See **slingshot** for synonyms. 2. old nautical slang, to abduct a man against his will and force him to become part of a ship's crew. Hence, to compel someone to do something they do not wish to. In Australian prisons this term is used specifically to refer to transferring prisoners to another jail without any prior warning. This is generally done as an unofficial form of punishment. Hence, as a noun, an unexpected transfer to another jail.

shark bait one who swims where there is danger of a shark attack.

sharpie a teenage or young adult hoodlum of the late 1960s and 1970s. Developed from the **bodgies** of the 1950s and early 1960s. Generally

sheila used of males, but also of females.

sheila a woman. *A couple of sheilas told me to get lost*. In use since the 1830s in Australia. Also common in NZ and even used in Britain in the late 19th century. It is a generic use of the common Irish girl's name. Sheila is basically a bloke's word – women on the whole do not use it. Some men seem to think it is a neutral word, rather than a derogatory one, and formerly this may have been closer to the truth, but nowadays women in general don't much like being called sheilas.

she'll be right everything will be okay.

a shingle short lacking a full complement of intelligence; mentally deranged. The 'shingle' in question is a wooden roofing tile, thus, in full it is 'a shingle short of a roof'. Aussie slang dating from the 1840s, making it one of the very earliest expressions of this sort. For similar comparisons see the entry for **short of**.

shivoo a party or celebration. Aussie slang since the 1830s. In origin an alteration of French *chez vous* 'at your place'.

shocker something dreadfully bad. Commonly used in sport for a bad game. *Had a shocker last Saturday*. Known in rhyming slang as a **Barry Crocker** (from the name of the Australian popular entertainer).

shonk a dishonest person; a swindler or con artist.

shoot through like a Bondi tram to depart in haste. Originally Sydney slang dating back to the 1940s, and referring to the trams along the Bondi line which were notoriously fast. Sydney's trams were discontinued in 1961, but the term remains. Now known and used the country over.

short of Since the 19th century people who are 'not all there' have been described by phrases comparing them metaphorically to some aggregate which is lacking its full complement. One of the earliest examples of this is the Australian phrase **a shingle short** (of a roof, that is). This dates back to the 1840s. And, an early British example of similar age is **a button short** (of a coat). A similar notion is found in **not the full quid**. Generally things are a 'few' or 'couple' short, as a **few bricks short of a load** or a **couple of alps short of a range** or a **few**

sheep short of a paddock. For some reason, food metaphors are the most common, such as a **few bites short of a bickie**, or **bangers short of a barbie**, a **couple of lamingtons short of a CWA meeting**, or **sandwiches short of a picnic**, or a **few Tim Tams short of a packet**.

shout **1.** to buy a round of drinks. Aussie slang dating back to the 1850s. Obviously Australian pubs have long been noisy places. Hence, a round of drinks bought for the present company. Someone who **wouldn't shout if a shark bit him** is a stingy bastard who won't buy drinks for others. **2.** hence, to pay for something for another person. *I'll shout you lunch.*

shrimp **1.** a diminutive or insignificant person. **2.** NOT the Aussie word for 'prawn'.

sickie a phoney sick day taken off work. Can be used to refer to genuine sick days as well, but that certainly isn't the most common usage.

sicko a disturbingly depraved person.

silent cop a circular steel traffic dome placed at intersections.

silly as... very silly. Australians have been quite inventive in coining silly phrases, such as **silly as a pork chop** (I've yet to get an intelligent conversation out of a pork chop), **silly as a two-bob watch** (that is, a wristwatch which only cost two bob to buy and not likely to keep good time), and **silly as three wet hens in a row**.

silvertail a derogatory term for a person from the upper crust of society.

since Archer won the Cup in a long, long time. Referring, of course, to the great racehorse Archer who won the inaugural Melbourne Cup back in 1861. If you want to go even further back in time you can say **since Adam was a pup**.

sink to drink down (a glass of booze). *Time to sink a few middies.* Great Aussie drinking slang since the 1910s. Also common in NZ.

skeg a derogatory term for a surfie. It derives from *skeg* 'the fin of a surfboard'. Also called a **skeg head**.

skip a derogatory term for an Anglo-Celtic Australian, as opposed to a person of Mediterranean or Arabic descent. A shortening of **skippy**.

skip hop Australian hip-hop or rap music.

skippy the fuller form of **skip**. Obviously it is derived from Skippy the Bush Kangaroo (from the 1960s TV series of the same name).

slab **1.** a carboard carton of two dozen cans or stubbies of beer. Aussie slang from the 1980s. **2.** a thousand dollars.

sledging the practice of heaping abuse and ridicule on members of the opposing team in an effort to upset their game. Originally Aussie cricket slang from the 1970s, from where it has spread to other sports. The practice is, of course, as old as the game of cricket and there are laws against it dating as far back as 1744.

sling off to disparage. *He was slinging off at his teachers.*

slingshot a child's catapult, typically made from a forked stick and rubber bands. Originally British slang. Also called a **dinger**, a **ging** (formerly widespread but not now, most common in WA and Qld), a **gonk** (restricted to north coast NSW) or a **shanghai**.

slot a prison cell. Hence, to lock someone up.

slouch hat the iconic hat of the Australian soldier. A wide-brimmed, rabbit-felt hat, usually worn with one side of the brim pinned up. Known officially as 'hat, fur felt, troops for the use of'.

sluggos speedos. Also called **sluggies**, **sluggers**, or **slug-huggers**. Referring to the revealing of the shape of the underlying penis. There are a host of slang terms for tight-fitting, and thus revealing, men's swimwear. These include **ball huggers**, **boasters**, **budgie smugglers** or **budgie huggers**, **cluster busters**, **cock chokers**, **cock jocks** (or **CJs**), **cod jocks**, **dick bathers**, **dick daks**, **dick pointers** or **dick pokers** (both shortened to **DPs**) and, especially in NSW, **dick stickers**. In Qld they are more commonly called **dick togs** (or, in front of grandma, **DTs**). You might think that is enough, but no – there are also **dipsticks**, **fish frighteners**, **knobbies**, **lolly bags**, **meat hangers** and **toolies**. An old-fashioned term, little heard nowadays, was **nylon disgusters**. Surfies, who wear boardies, call them **clubbies**, referring to the preferences of surf lifesavers. And they also get called **racers**, as they are used for competitive swimming, and, in NSW, **scungies**, from their similarity to underwear.

sly grog illicitly made or supplied alcoholic liquor. Aussie slang since the 1820s. Hence, a person who supplied alcohol illegally was known as a **sly grogger**, and the place where it was obtained was called a **sly groggery** or **sly grog joint**.

smoke-oh a rest from work; a tea-break or the like. Australian slang since the 1860s. Originally short for a 'smoking break'. Also spelt **smoke-o** or **smoko**.

snag a sausage.

snagger a poor shearer. Recorded since the 1880s, it appears to have been first used to refer to shearers who were learning the trade and sheared less than 50 sheep a day. Eventually came to mean a poor or slow shearer who wasn't a beginner, or a man who was once a good shearer, but is now old and content to jog along with 100 or so sheep a day. In the song *Click Go the Shears* the snagger beats the ringer (the fastest shearer in the shed) by one stroke: 'The ringer looks around and is beaten by a blow/And he curses the old snagger with the bare-bellied yoe'.

Snake Gully a mythical remote place in the outback.

snot block a chiefly Victorian term for a vanilla slice. Also called a **snot box** or a **snot brick**.

snow man an old paper $100 note. Because it sported a picture of Antarctic explorer Douglas Mawson. Now replaced by the **green giant** (see entry).

sook a wimpish, overly sensitive person; a cry-baby.

sort a good-looking woman. *There were some real sorts at the party*. When unqualified it always means attractive, but it is very commonly used with a qualifying adjective, either positive, as in *great sort* or *top sort*, or with a negative one, as in *rough sort* or *drack sort*.

spanner water extremely cold water. Because when blokes go swimming – it 'tightens the nuts'.

Speed Gordon the name under which American comic superhero Flash Gordon was for a long time known in Australia. Hence the slang phrase **in more trouble than Speed Gordon** – in other words, in a lot of strife. Back in the 1930s and 40s, when Flash Gordon was first published in Australia, the word *flash* most commonly meant 'ostentatious or showy', and so a figure called 'Flash' Gordon would be expected to be a bit of a lair. Hence the renaming.

spinebash to lie down and rest or sleep; to loaf on the job. Hence, a rest or slumber. Formed from the earlier phrase **bash the spine** (see entry).

spit chips to vent spleen. This originally meant to be in dire need of a drink, that is, your mouth was so dry that if you spat, wood chips came out. Nowadays the metaphor seems to be one of being so angry that you could chew up a log of wood and spit out chips.

spud 1. a potato. An old word dating back to the mid-19th century. Recorded earliest in NZ, but known to be used in Australia from at least the 1890s. 2. a hole in a sock through which the skin shows. 3. a fist. Hence, **spuds** is another name for the game rock, paper, scissors. To **spud** someone is to challenge them to a game of spuds. *I'll spud you to see who goes first*.

spunk a good-looking person, male or female. Aussie slang since the 1970s. Also known as a **spunk bubble**, **spunk bucket** or **spunk rat**, and, for the ladies only, a **spunkette**. Originally *spunk* was British slang meaning 'semen', an old term dating back to the 1860s. In fact, in Britain this is still the current meaning and thus it can cause some confusion and embarrassment to visiting Poms.

spunky 1. good-looking; attractive; drop-dead gorgeous. Hence, **spunkiness**, the quality of being a spunk. 2. a good-looking person, male or female. *There were heaps of spunkies down the flicks last night*. This is the earliest sense, dating back to the 1960s. Not so common anymore.

squashed fly biscuit a biscuit with dried fruit between two thin layers of sweet pastry; also called a **dead fly biscuit** or a **fly cemetery**.

squib 1. a racehorse or greyhound that starts well but finishes terribly. Also called a **damp squib**. From *squib* for a type of firecracker – a damp one doesn't go off. 2. a coward. Hence, to **squib it** is to act in a cowardly fashion; to pike out.

squiz a quick but close look. Perhaps a blend of *squint* and *quiz*. Hence, to look at quickly but closely.

stack on to produce or put something on. *They really*

stack on a great party. Commonly in the phrases **stack on an act** or **stack on a turn** meaning to make an appalling big fuss over nothing, and **stack on a blue** meaning to start a fight.

starver a saveloy.

starve the lizards! Heavens above! Good lord! Great Aussie exclamation of surprise or exasperation. Occasionally in the form **stiffen the lizards!** First recorded back in the 1920s. Little heard these days, especially not used by city folk. See the similar expression **stone the crows!**

Steak and Kidney rhyming slang for 'Sydney'. First recorded way back in 1905.

St Georges Terrace cocky in WA, a person who owns a country property, often for purposes of tax avoidance, but who lives and works in Perth.

sticker licker in SA, a parking inspector. See **brown bomber** for the full set of regionalisms.

the sticks 1. any remote region far from civilisation; the outback. 2. in Aussie Rules, the goal posts.

stickybeak 1. an inquisitive, prying person. Hence, as a verb, to pry or meddle, to stick your nose in where it isn't wanted. 2. a look merely to satisfy your own inquisitiveness. *We went to the inspection just to have a stickybeak.* Commonly shortened to **sticky**. *Have a sticky at this.*

stiffen the crows! Heavens above! Good lord! A variant of **stone the crows!** First recorded in the 1930s. Similar is **stiffen the lizards!** and the uncommon **stiffen the wombats!**

stir to taunt, tease or needle, especially just for the fun of it. Probably a shortening of 'stir the possum', which is recorded much earlier.

stir the possum to create a disturbance or uproar. A sleeping possum does not take well to being stirred up.

stoked amazed, thrilled, delighted, blown away. Common term among surfies.

stone the crows! Heavens above! Good lord! Great Aussie exclamation of surprise or exasperation. Dates back to the 1920s. One classic saying that is sadly dying out. Similar phrases, also on the verge of extinction, are **stiffen the crows!** and **starve the lizards!**

stoush **1.** a fight or brawl; hence, an argument or altercation. Aussie slang since the 1890s. Perhaps originating from Scottish dialect *stash* 'a commotion or quarrel'. Used by soldiers to refer to war or a battle. World War I was commonly known as **the Big Stoush**. **2.** as a verb, to fight with someone; to hit or bash someone.

streaker's excuse the time-worn excuse 'It seemed like a good idea at the time.' This term got its name on Easter Sunday of 1974 when Dave Cook and Allana Kereopa streaked down the straight at Sydney's Royal Randwick Racecourse during the Doncaster Handicap. When caught and questioned as to why they had done this Allana replied 'It seemed like a good idea at the time.'

strewth! My God! Good lord! Heavens above! Hell's bells! Actually originally British, but recorded in Australia since the beginning of the 1900s, and iconically Australian. In origin a shortened form of the exclamation *God's truth!* Also commonly spelt **struth!**

strike a light! an exclamation of surprise. First recorded in the 1920s. Australians have been particularly adept at coining variations on this theme in which you call on God to visit increasingly ridiculous punishments on you. Aussie originals – with their earliest known dates include **strike me blue** (1902), **dead** (1932), **fat** (1895), **handsome** (1955), **pink** (1892), **purple** (1904), and **roan** (1917). The British form **strike me lucky** is also used here. These can all be shortened to simply **strike me!** Or, with even greater brevity, to the simple **strike!**

Strine characteristic spoken Australian English – what linguists call 'broad Australian' – that is, the type spoken by country folk and ockers, not university professors, politicians and the well-to-do. *He wouldn't know what a dunny is, he doesn't talk Strine!* Coined by Alastair Morrison and made popular in 1965 through his book *Let Stalk Strine* (=let's talk 'Stralian). Posing as 'Afferbeck Lauder' (=alphabetical order), Professor of Strine Studies at Ezz Rock, Morrison set about re-spelling perfectly ordinary words and phrases into seemingly meaningless gobbledegook that was only understood once you read it out loud. Examples include **Gloria Soame** for *glorious home*; **laze and gem** for *ladies and gentlemen*;

muncer go for *months ago*; **sly drool** for *slide rule*; and (the most renowned and oft quoted example) **Emma Chisit** for *How much is it?* Now used affectionately for Australian English generally.

stubby a small, squat beer bottle.

suicide season in the tropical north, the approach of the Wet. Causes extreme tension and irritability.

sunbeam a plate or utensil which was laid out but not used at a meal and hence does not need to be washed up. Compare **moonbeam**.

super full-strength beer, as opposed to **unleaded**. Also used for other 'full-strength' items, such as cola containing caffeine.

surfie a devotee of surfboard riding; one who lives the life of a surfer – sun-bleached hair, tanned hide, waxed feet. The Americans use the term **surfer** – but actually this is originally Australian as well. Of course, back then it didn't refer to surfboard riding, but rather to what used to be called 'surf-bathing' – that is, swimming in the surf and bodysurfing.

surfie chick a female who is part of the surfie subculture.

swag **1.** a bundle or a blanket-roll containing personal belongings and useful items carried by a traveller through the bush or by an itinerant looking for work. The defining feature of the **swagman**. Also commonly called a **bluey** or, less commonly, a **Matilda** or **shiralee**. First recorded in the 1840s in Australia and the 1850s in New Zealand. **2.** a bedroll, without belongings; hence, a traveller's bedding unrolled for sleeping in. *We hopped into our swags right away as the night was already cold.* **3.** an unspecified but large number or quantity. *There was a swag of people at the meeting.*

swagman a man who travels about the country on foot, carrying his possessions in a swag and living on his earnings from occasional jobs, or gifts of money or food. First recorded in the 1860s and since the 1890s commonly shortened to **swaggie**. The term was also in common use in New Zealand, but there it was generally shortened to *swagger* rather than *swaggie*. The era of swagmen, at its height during the Great Depression, came to an end with World War II, but the swagman has lived on in Australian cultural history, and is the central figure of

sweet

Australia's national song, *Waltzing Matilda*. A female itinerant was, of course, known as a **swagwoman** – but these were always rare.

sweet all right, okay, in order. *Don't worry mate – everything's sweet*.

swiftie a con job or swindle.

Sydney or the bush! all or nothing, as in making a do-or-die attempt, gambling against the odds, or the like.

T

tallie in Qld, a 750ml bottle of beer. Generally called a **long neck** elsewhere, except WA, where the term **king brown** is favoured.

tall poppy a person who is pre-eminent in a particular field; a person with great status. Australians in general have a bit of a negative view of tall poppies, especially if they seem to get above themselves. When this happens they need to be cut down to size. The Aussie penchant for such pruning is known as the **tall poppy syndrome**.

Tasmaniac an inhabitant of Tasmania.

Tassie colloquial rendering of Tasmania.

teacher arms the arms of an overweight or matronly woman, having flabby triceps.

technicolour yawn the act of vomiting. A term dear to and principally spread by Barry Humphries.

Territory confetti ring pulls from beer cans.

Territory rig formal attire in the Top End. See **Darwin rig** for an explanation.

thingo Aussie way of saying 'thingummy' or 'thingamyjigget' or 'thingamabob' or even 'thingy'. It has been in common use since the 1960s.

things are crook in Tallarook The situation is not good. This is more common in Victoria, the home state of Tallarook. In NSW things tend to be crook in either **Muswellbrook** or **Coolongolook**.

thugby a derogatory term used by AFL folk for Rugby Union or Rugby League.

tickle the peter to rob the till.

tilly in Qld and rural northern NSW, a ute. Using the middle bit of the word *utility*, rather than the front end.

Tim Tam slam a culinary treat in which two diagonally opposite corners of an Arnott's Tim Tam biscuit are bitten off and hot coffee is then sucked through the biscuit via these openings. At a certain critical point the whole biscuit must be deftly tossed into the mouth, otherwise it disintegrates in your hands. Also called the **Tim Tam suck** or a **Tim Tam straw**.

tin lid Aussie rhyming slang for 'kid'. This dates way back to 1905.

tinnie 1. a can of beer. If you are **a few tinnies short of a slab**, then you are not very smart. 2. a light, aluminium-hulled boat.

tizz up to dress up in glamorous fashion. Also in the form **tizzy up**.

the Toaster a derisive nickname for the apartment and retail building running along East Circular Quay, Sydney.

toey 1. of a racehorse, eager to run. 2. anxious, apprehensive, edgy. If you are really toey then you could be described as **toey as a Roman sandal**. 3. fast, speedy.

Toorak tractor a city-only 4WD that never sees off-road conditions, principally used for shopping and shuttling kids to and from school. Also called a **Toorak taxi**. Originally Melbourne slang this derogatory term has spread throughout the entire country and is the most common of all the variants, all based on the names of affluent suburbs. Perth has the **Dalkeith tractor**, Adelaide the **Burnside warrior**, and Brisbane the **Kenmore tractor**. In Sydney the terms are legion, including **Balmain bulldozer**, **Balmoral bulldozer**, **Bronte buggy**, **Double Bay tractor**, **Mosman tractor**, **North Shore tank**, **Rose Bay shopping trolley** and **Turramurra tractor**.

toot a toilet or dunny. In origin perhaps an alteration of *toilet*.

Top End the northern part of the Northern Territory. Hence, a **Top Ender** is a person living in the Top End.

t'othersider in WA, a person living on the other side of the Nullarbor Plain.

townie one who comes from a town and is ignorant of country ways. Aussie slang since the 1820s.

track the open road; hence, to be **on the track** meant to be travelling as a swagman. Also known as the **wallaby track**.

the Track the Stuart Highway running between Darwin and Alice Springs. To go **down the Track** is to go south from Darwin, and naturally, to go **up the Track** is to go north from the Alice.

trackie tracksuit, as in **trackie pants** or **trackie top**, and, of course, **trackie daks** are tracksuit pants. Hence, **trackies**, a tracksuit. *I spent all morning in me trackies.*

trammie a tram conductor or driver.

the traps any place you frequent. *I've seen him around the traps.* Originally referring to a route along which a person had laid traps which they then habitually visited to collect the game that had been caught.

traveller a can or bottle of beer consumed while driving; a roadie.

treadly a bicycle. Aussie slang. A kid's word since the 1960s. Also called a **deadly treadly** (see entry).

triantelope a huntsman spider. Venerable Aussie slang dating back to the 1840s. Also called a **trantylope**.

triantiwontigongolope a mythical insect or beastie. Sometimes portrayed as a dreadfully dangerous bunyip-like creature in order to frighten children or naive city folk visiting the bush. Coined by CJ Dennis in his *A Book For Kids*, 1921. Commonly bastardised into forms having less syllables, as *triantiwontygong*, *triantiwontigog*, *triantimontygoggle* and *trianiwonigong*.

troppo mentally disturbed. Originally World War II Aussie slang, referring to mental illness resulting from long military service in the tropics. Especially common in the phrase **go troppo**.

truckie a truck or semi-trailer driver. Excellent Aussie slang first recorded way back in 1919, but becoming really common from the 1950s onwards.

true blue 1. genuine; fair dinkum. *They were true blue bushies from the outback.* 2. fair dinkum Aussie. *She's true blue.* 3. as a noun, an Australian. *You're a true blue now.*

tucker great Aussie slang for food. *It's time for tucker.* Has been in constant use since the 1850s. Originally meaning a meal, that is, something to be tucked away (in the stomach).

tucker bag a bag used for carrying food, as by a swagman.

tucker box a box for carrying a food supply. The most famous of all such boxes is the one at Five Mile, just outside Gundagai, NSW. The story goes that a drover left his trusty dog to guard his tucker box while he went off on an errand, but, through some fatal misadventure, he never returned and the faithful dog remained on guard until its own death. Since 1932 the dog on the tucker box has been commemorated in the form of a statue at Five Mile. Interestingly, this legend only arose to explain a bowdlerised form of an old folk song. In the original song the dog 'shat in the tucker box', to the chagrin of the owner and the amusement of his fellows. This was a little too rude for decent ears, and so 'sat on' was substituted for 'shat in'.

tucker out to weary, tire, exhaust.

tuckshop arms the arms of an overweight or matronly woman with flabby triceps.

Turramurra tractor Sydney slang, a derogatory term for a city-only 4WD. See **Toorak tractor** for a host of synonyms.

two bob 1. old slang term for a florin or two shilling coin. Transferred to twenty cents after the introduction of decimal currency in 1966. Used in many colloquial expressions. To **have two bob each way** is to hedge your bets. If you're **not the full two bob**, then you're a bit slow. Something of little worth is **not worth two bob**. And your **two bob's worth** is an old Aussie version of the usual 'two cents worth'. 2. a circular pattern made on the ground by driving a car in a tight circle at high speed and causing the rear wheels to skid; a doughnut.

two-bob lair a cheap, flashy lair.

two-bob watch a cheap and crappy watch, literally, one that only cost two bob. Commonly used as a simile for dysfunctional people or things. You can be **silly as a two-bob watch**, or **mad as a two-bob watch**, or **bent as a two-bob watch**. If your car doesn't run well, then it **goes like a two-bob watch**. And, if someone is stacking on a turn, then they are **carrying on like a two-bob watch**.

two-up the classic Australian gambling game in which two coins are thrown off a kip into the air so that they spin. Bets are laid on whether they fall heads or tails – a fall of one head and one tail requiring the coins to be tossed again. Also called **swy** or the **national game**. The term is first recorded back in 1884, and for most of its life the game has been illegal. It was popular with soldiers in World War I and thus became an Anzac Day staple, generally tolerated by the law, and finally made legal for that day alone. Two-up is now also legal in casinos and a few two-up schools in country towns where it is sanctioned as a tourist attraction.

U

uey a U-turn. To take a U-turn you either **chuck a uey** or **hang a uey**. While everyone says it, no-one is really sure how to spell this great Aussie word. Other efforts have been **u-ie**, **uee**, and even **youee**.

uggies colloquial shortening of **ugg boots** – which is now a term trademarked by an American company in America. The Australian ugg boot won its case however and it remains a generic term here. The origin of the term is not clear. One suggestion is that it is short for *ugly boot*.

unco awkward or clumsy. Short for 'uncoordinated'. *That was an unco thing to do.* Hence, a clumsy person. Also known as **The Man From Unco**. A common term used by schoolkids.

underdaks underpants. From **daks** meaning pants. Also called **underchunders** or **underdungers**.

underground mutton rabbit meat used as food.

unleaded low-alcohol beer, as opposed to **super**. Also applied to caffeine-free cola, and the like.

up a gumtree in all sorts of strife.

up the duff pregnant. Probably from old slang *duff* = pudding, as in 'in the pudding club'.

up there Cazaly a cry of encouragement, especially at the AFL. Originally a cry directed at Aussie Rules legend Roy Cazaly.

useful as ... Australians have been diligent in coining ironic phrases to denote the completely useless. Firstly, there are those with a rural flavour. Such as **useful as a bucket under a bull, a dead dingo's donger, a dry thunderstorm, a sore arse to a boundary rider, a wether at a ram sale, tits on a bull**, or **two knobs of billy-goat poop**. Then there are anatomical similes, including **useful as a witch's tit, a wart on the hip** or **a third armpit**. Other phrases tend to associate objects that functionally don't go together, such as **useful as a glass door on a dunny, a pocket on a singlet, a roo bar on a skateboard, a**

useful as a submarine with screen doors

submarine with screen doors, a glass eye at a key hole, and **an ashtray on a motorbike**. Finally, there are those that refer to things out of place, to wit: **useful as a nun at a buck's night**, **a pork chop at a Jewish barbecue**, or **a tart at a christening**.

ute a utility truck or utility van. In Qld and northern NSW, it is more commonly termed a **tilly**.

V

VB shoulder a sore shoulder resulting from habitual carrying of cases of Victoria Bitter beer.

veeb Victoria Bitter beer; a glass, can or bottle of this. Also **veebers**.

Vee Dub a Volkswagen car.

Vegemite a thick, black paste, a yeast extract with tons of salt, beloved by all true blue Aussies. In the early 1920s American Dr Cyril P. Callister, working for the Fred Walker Company, later bought by Kraft Foods Limited, invented this iconic Australian food. In 1923 a national contest was held in Australia to find the spread a name, and Fred Walker's daughter chose Vegemite from hundreds of entries. As initial sales were sluggish, due in part to the popularity of the similar British product Marmite, Walker tried to rename Vegemite to 'Parwill' – that is, 'Marmite, but Parwill' (Ma might, but Pa will!). This marketing ploy was tried out in Qld only, but it failed and Vegemite returned to its original name. Of course, Kraft is an American company, but – ah-hem – it's un-Australian to think about that fact when eating Vegemite! In terms of slang, Vegemite is used in the phrase **happy little vegemite**, used to refer to someone in a good mood. This stems from a Vegemite radio advertising jingle that first hit Australian airwaves in 1954. Also, **little vegemite** has come to mean a child. Thus you can have a *clever little vegemite* or a *top little vegemite* or a *good little vegemite*. It's always a positive thing to be a little vegemite.

vegie 1. vegetable. *He's dug a little vegie patch.* Hence, **vegies**, vegetables. *No ice-cream till you eat all your vegies.* 2. of school subjects, of the lowest academic standard. *I'm only doing vegie maths.*

voice like a ... Someone with an unpleasant, rasping voice is said to have a **voice like a chain being**

dragged through gravel. An even harsher voice is described as being **like a chainsaw hitting granite**. Other poetic descriptions of vocal cacophony are a **voice like a strangled fowl**, a **voice like a billygoat sitting on tin** and a **voice like a knife that has been left stuck in a lemon too long**. Compare **head like a ....**

Wallaby Bob's cousin ruined, wrecked, rooted (get it? *Roo Ted* is Wallaby Bob's cousin). *Man I am feeling like Wallaby Bob's cousin.* Also heard in the form **Wallaby Bobbed**, as in *I'm a bit Wallaby Bobbed at the moment.*

wallaby track the open road as formerly used by swagmen. Also simply called **the wallaby**. Hence, **on the wallaby**, living as a swagman looking for work.

walloper a police officer – as viewed by those on the receiving end.

waltzing Matilda travelling on foot with a swag to look for work. See **Matilda** for more information.

waxhead a derogatory term for a surfie. So called in reference to the wax used on surfboards. Also shortened to **waxie**.

wedding tackle the male genitalia.

wedge a beer bought between shouts; a tweenie. *Gibbo couldn't wait for the next round, so he had a wedge.*

wee juggler a Major Mitchell cockatoo. A beautiful example of the 'Law of Hobson-Jobson' at work in Australia. The Law of Hobson-Jobson is the linguistic process whereby a word borrowed from one language is changed so that it resembles words in another language. Of course Major Mitchell cockatoos are not small birds that can juggle. The word is a corruption of the word *wijugula*, the name of the bird in the Aboriginal language Wiradjuri, from central NSW.

Werribee trout Melbourne slang for a floating piece of human excrement in the ocean. See **blind mullet** for a swag of synonyms.

westie your typical Aussie yobbo type – mullet haircut, flannos and jeans, from the low socio-economic stratum. Originally a derogatory term for a person from the western suburbs of Sydney. In Sydney, **westie** is applied disparagingly to any person living west of your own suburb – thus a Bondi inhabitant may call a person from Ryde a westie, but Ryde inhabitants would not consider themselves as such, and instead apply the term to people from Parramatta, who in turn apply it to people from Penrith, and so on. Only inner city trendies and residents of beachy suburbs are not ever labelled westies. As a general rule of thumb, the typical westie features become more prominent the further you move west from Sydney's centre – though, that is also true the further you go north and south. First recorded in the 1970s, **westie** has now spread to most of NSW, and is even used in Ballarat where the less affluent part of town is to the west.

whacker a stupid person; an eccentric or weirdo.

wharfie a dock worker.

whinger an inveterate complainer; a nark who's always got something to grumble about.

whip-around an impromptu collection of money for a

wee juggler

present, farewell, good cause, etc.

whip the cat to vent frustration over something that can't be changed; to cry over spilt milk. An Aussie slang expression since the 1840s.

whirly-whirly a miniature whirlwind that picks up dust and rubbish – common in the outback. Also called a **whirlywind**, especially in Qld.

white-ant 1. to undermine a person, organisation or enterprise. 2. to move in on your best friend's girlfriend.

white can 1. a can of Carlton Draught beer. 2. a can of Swan Light beer. As opposed to a **blue**, **green**, **red** or **yellow can** (see entries).

white maggot a derogatory term for an Aussie Rules umpire.

white rabbits among kids, a phrase to invoke immunity from being punched. Especially used on the first day of any month with the letter 'r' in its name – failure to say it can result in your being punched repeatedly until you do. This is an old British folk tradition brought to Australia. Another use is when sitting around a camp fire – if the smoke is blowing in your face you say 'I hate white rabbits' to make the smoke change direction.

the whole box and dice everything; the whole kit and caboodle.

who's robbing this coach? Who is in charge here? A rhetorical question meaning 'Stay out of it!' The story goes that Ned Kelly was bailing up a coach one day and proclaimed 'I'm going to rob all the men and take all the women'. To which one of the male passengers said, 'You can't do that, you dreadful man', only to be shouted down by a female passenger saying, 'Who's robbing this coach, you or Mister Kelly?' Clearly apocryphal, but why ruin a good story with the truth?

wide brown land Australia. From the 1908 poem *My Country* by Dorothea Mackellar.

widgie in the 1950s and 60s, a teenage female delinquent; the counterpart of the **bodgie**. Widgies were especially noted for wild behaviour and free sexuality, and for dressing in tight, revealing skirts and sweaters, and having short, duck-tailed haircuts. The origin of the term is a bit of a mystery. One theory is that it is a blend of the words *women* and *bodgie*, but this doesn't have the ring of truth about it. Another more charming solution is that it referred to the hairstyle which had a vee or *wedge* at the back – it is but a small step from *wedgie* to *widgie*.

willy-willy a miniature whirlwind that picks up dust and rubbish, common in the outback. Recorded from the 1890s. From the Aboriginal language Yindjibarndi of the Fortescue River district of WA. Compare **cockeyed bob**.

wombat someone who is slow-moving or slow-witted. So called after the well-known nocturnal, burrowing marsupial. The word itself comes from the extinct Aboriginal language of the Sydney region, Dharug.

wombat-headed dull, stupid, block-headed. A great Aussie insult originated by Ned Kelly in his famous Jerilderie letter of 1879. Ned asked: 'Is my brothers and sisters and my mother not to be pitied also who has no alternative only to put up with the brutal and cowardly conduct of a parcel of big ugly fat-necked wombat-headed big-bellied magpie-legged narrow-hipped splaw-footed sons of Irish Bailiffs or English landlords which is better known as Officers of Justice or Victorian Police?'

Woop Woop an imaginary town or district that is extremely remote. First recorded back in 1918 and formed by duplicating a sound, like many Aussie placenames of Aboriginal origin. Back in the 1920s there was a sawmill named Woop Woop about 10 km from Wilga, in south-west WA. It was established in 1925, and it is believed the name is derived from the sound made by frogs common in the area. The New Zealand version of this is **the wop wops**, which has been around since the 1950s.

worker's crack bum cleavage showing above a worker's low-slung stubbies.

work like a drover's pup to work your heart out.

wouldn't be dead for quids an Aussie expression of lust for life.

wouldn't work in an iron lung a phrase describing a completely lazy person. The notion is that even if something else was doing the breathing for them, they wouldn't work.

wowser a killjoy, spoilsport or nark; a person who doesn't

wowser

know how to have fun and wishes to prevent others from doing so; a puritanical prude who publicly complains about other people's behaviour; a no-good do-gooder. It first appears in the 1890s in the Sydney *Truth* newspaper and was later claimed by the editor John Norton to be of his own coinage – from the slogan *We Only Want Social Evils Remedied*. However, some correspondents to that paper at the time denied Norton's claim.

XYZ a polite aside informing someone that their fly is undone. Standing for 'eXamine Your Zipper'.

yabber to talk or chat; to chatter or rabbit on. *Stop yabbering will ya?* Aussie slang since the 1840s, from an Aboriginal language. Hence, a conversation. *We had a bit of a yabber about it.*

yacker talk or chatter. *There was a lot of yacker going on.* Hence, as a verb, to chat. Not to be confused with **yakka**.

yakka hard work, especially manual labour. Aussie slang since the 1880s and coming from the Aboriginal language Yagara, from the Brisbane region. Now most commonly found in the collocation **hard yakka**, or in the phrase **all yack and no yakka**, used to describe someone who's always talking about what they're going to do instead of doing it.

yarn **1.** a talk or chat. *We were just having a quiet yarn about old times.* Amazing as it may seem, this meaning is peculiar to Australia and New Zealand. The verb use, to chat or gossip, is also common in Oz and NZ, but is also used elsewhere. **2.** an exaggerated story or tale, especially a long one about extraordinary events. Hence, to tell stories or tall tales.

Yarra banker a soapbox orator on the banks of the Yarra.

the Yartz the Strine pronunciation of 'the Arts'.

yellow can a can of Castlemaine XXXX beer. As opposed to a

yike

blue, green, red or white can (see entries).

yike a brawl or argument. Origin unknown.

YMCA dinner a meal made from leftovers. Standing for *Yesterday's Muck Cooked Again.*

yodel to vomit.

you beaut! a cry of joyful praise. Also common in the form **you little beaut!** or **you little beauty!**

you'll do a great Aussie compliment. *He had muscles on his muscles and thighs like tree trunks. I looked at him and said 'You'll do'.*

your blood's worth bottling you are a fantastic person; you're a legend.

youse **1.** a common Aussie plural form of the second person pronoun 'you'. *Where are youse two going?* Sometimes spelt **yous**, and also **yers** or **yas**. First recorded back in the 1890s, this is a borrowing from Irish English, where it is usually spelt *yez*. It is interesting to note that Irish Gaelic did have a separate plural for the form of the second person pronoun, and thus it is only sensible that they created one in their own variety of English. **2.** also used as a singular form of 'you'. *I ain't afraid of youse.* This seems to appear in the 1910s.

Z

zambuck a St John Ambulance officer. Old slang dating back to the 1910s. So called after the proprietary name of an antiseptic ointment they commonly used.

zizz a nap or sleep. From the cartoonist's *zzz*, representing of the sound of snoring.

MACQUARIE DICTIONARY ONLINE

www.macquariedictionary.com.au

Subscribe to the complete *Macquarie Dictionary* online, updated annually with new words and definitions.

Use Drag & Drop to get instant definitions from the *Macquarie*.

Also available online is the full *Macquarie Thesaurus* – that perfect word is just a click away.

MACQUARIE
Australia's national dictionary